# SMART DIVORCE

Lee Rosen
and
Lisa Angel

Morgan and Dawson Publishing

RALEIGH, NC

Lee Rosen & Lisa Angel/Morgan & Dawson Publishing
4101 Lake Boone Trail
Raleigh, NC
27607
MorganandDawson.com

Lisa Angel
Board Certified Family Law Specialist
angel@rosen.com

Lee Rosen
Rosen Law Firm
rosen@rosen.com

Ordering Information:
Quantity sales. Special discounts are available on quantity purchases by corporations, associations, and others. For details, contact the Morgan & Dawson Publishing at publisher@morgananddawson.com

Smart Divorce/ Lee Rosen & Lisa Angel. —2nd ed.
ISBN 10: 0-9893701-4-3
ISBN 13: 978-0-9893701-4-1

# Contents

## Part Two: The Major Divorce Decisions

## Part Three: The Best Way to Complete Your Divorce

## Part Four: After the Divorce

# Introduction

Divorce doesn't have to be devastating. Reject the idea that you'll be damaged by the process. In fact, if you do it right, you'll grow from the experience. You'll start your new life better than you were before.

Divorce is difficult. There's no avoiding the emotional, financial, and legal challenges associated with divorce. Each member of the family will be marked by the experience in one way or another.

What we've learned, through working with thousands of families going through divorce, is that some people come out of the experience devastated. They wallow in the aftermath for years. Their divorce impacts their day-to-day life for decades after the end of the marriage. Many of these people never let go of the negativity surrounding the end of their marriage.

Other people have a different experience of divorce. They bounce back. They cope with the process as it happens and then they recover. They move on to live bigger and better lives. They're happier, healthier, and more prosperous than in the past. They enter into new relationships, and they thrive. They don't deny the challenge presented by the divorce, but they don't let it define the rest of their lives.

How is it that people can be impacted so differently by a divorce?

We're not experts in psychology—we're lawyers. But, we've absorbed some lessons as we've observed our clients going through this process. We've found that some people learn from their divorce. They gain new insights. They turn the negatives into positives by maturing and evolving. We think they've figured out the way to divorce smartly.

We wrote this book to help you divorce in a smart way. We can't pass along all of the emotional lessons to be learned from going through an experience as difficult as divorce—that's better left to the mental health experts. We can, however, help you understand the legal issues. Knowing what's coming, and understanding it before it happens, will give you the emotional space required to grow from your own experience.

1

Staying one step ahead on the legal issues helps you avoid becoming overwhelmed. Knowing what's coming allows you to focus on the next step so you don't get rolled over by the process. With the knowledge you'll gain in this book, you'll be able to Divorce Smartly.

# Overview of the Book

Smart Divorce is a growth experience. It is said, "what doesn't kill you makes you stronger." This saying, made famous by Nietzsche, is certainly true of divorce. You'll survive and you'll grow stronger—we promise.

We'll make it easier for you cope with your divorce by making sure you understand the legal issues and anticipate each upcoming step. We'll prepare you for what's going to happen on the legal and financial fronts so you have the time and energy you need to deal with your emotional issues.

You'll quickly and efficiently move through the divorce process because you'll have a firm grasp on the legal and financial issues. Being well-prepared, you'll spend less time and money on the process. You'll experience less fear and feel energized to move on with your life.

*Smart Divorce* is organized around the phases of the process. Starting with the idea of preparing for divorce, we'll educate you about the upcoming steps and help you get organized. Then we move on to major divorce decisions, helping you think through your positions and decide these issues ahead of time so you'll never feel pressured.

We move from there to information on completing your divorce, where you will figure out the most effective way to put your ideas into action. The manner in which you handle the divorce impacts the cost, speed, and effectiveness of the process. We'll discuss all of your options. Finally, we'll talk about life after divorce. Yes, there is life after, and we'll help you move forward so you can enjoy it.

*Smart Divorce* is a great resource for helping you through your divorce. It's not, however, a substitute for a lawyer and expert legal advice. Specifically, we don't provide the details of the laws of any particular state. We provide you with a broad overview of divorce without delving into the specifics that will be explained by your lawyer. It's prudent to have a lawyer with whom you can work well on your team.

# Part One:
# Preparing for Divorce

# Before You Divorce

Divorce is a trauma. There's no way around that. Even when it is mutually agreed on, and obviously the right thing for everyone involved, ripping apart the life two people have woven is bound to be messy and painful.

Nearly half of all married couples will have to deal with divorce, but few go into the process with a clear sense of what is happening to them, or why. Even though we're all vaguely aware of the doom-and-gloom statistics regarding marriage in this day and age, all but the most cynical of couples marry expecting to stay together happily ever after. Once married, people generally don't think much about what divorce is like or how it would affect their lives unless they begin to experience major problems in the relationship.

Being naïve about divorce is a mistake: understanding what happens during divorce can lead to better decisions, smoother negotiations, faster settlements, and far fewer sleepless nights. This first chapter, with its big-picture perspective on the divorce process, is your starting point for learning the lessons of *your* divorce.

In this chapter, we answer many of the questions people have when they first begin thinking about ending a marriage. We consider the common causes of divorce to help spark insights about what went wrong. Perhaps you can even resolve your marital problems without going all the way down the divorce path. If not, developing an understanding of what happened may help you avoid repeating those mistakes in future relationships.

After considering the causes of divorce, we help you develop some realistic expectations about the often-misunderstood outcomes of divorce, including how divorce affects happiness, finances, and parenting. Understanding potential divorce ramifications will help you make a better decision about whether you should try to save your marriage. For those who are uncertain if divorce is their best choice, we discuss options you might want to try prior to, or instead of, divorce. Finally, if splitting up still seems to be the only viable option, this chapter will help you understand more about what you will have to deal with so you can make the transition as smoothly as possible.

At this early point we want to call special attention to domestic violence. Nearly one-third of women experience at least one physical assault by a partner during adulthood. The portion within married couples is lower, but some of the most serious problems occur when couples separate. If you are in a violent relationship, you need to skip ahead to our chapter on domestic violence right away. While most of the information in this book will prove relevant, there are a number of special considerations that survivors of domestic violence need to be aware of as soon as possible.

---

# The Causes of Divorce

Whether you are feeling lost in the throes of litigation, revisiting a decade-old custody arrangement, or considering a trial separation, we would challenge you with this question: How can you use this experience, right now, to grow as a person?

When faced with divorce, people naturally wonder how their lives took this unexpected turn. The question of what causes divorce has been hotly debated, especially since the divorce rate rose a few decades ago. Even so, there is no comprehensive list of causes. If we had a greater understanding of what causes divorce, it probably would not be so prevalent.

A survey conducted for the American Association of Retired Persons (AARP) asked those who divorced after age forty to identify, from a long list, the three major reasons for their divorce.[1] They chose:

- Verbal, physical, or emotional abuse (34 percent)
- Different values, lifestyles (29 percent)
- Cheating (27 percent)

- Simply fell out of love/no obvious problems (24 percent)
- Alcohol or drug abuse (21 percent)
- Being a control freak (16 percent)
- Money problems (14 percent)
- Not carrying their weight in the marriage (14 percent)
- Fell in love with someone else (10 percent)
- Abandonment (10 percent)

Many experts say that the answers people give in surveys such as this usually refer to symptoms rather than actual causes. For instance, cheating is usually a symptom of a relationship that has broken down. Such symptoms usually occur after some other change caused the relationship to deteriorate. Cheating may be the last straw that leads to the divorce. In most cases, though, the point that causes the final collapse of the marriage occurs after at least one spouse, but usually both, has lived with years of unhappiness in the marriage.

So, if what we commonly think of as causes of divorce are just symptoms, what are the real causes? Experts who have studied the issue say that communication problems, particularly when it comes to resolving conflict, underlie most divorces.

Dr. John Gottman, perhaps the most respected and dedicated researcher of these issues, has found evidence that *what* a couple fights about is not nearly as important as the *how* they fight. He has also shown that happily married couples don't necessarily have less conflict than those who divorce. Dr. Gottman has identified key behaviors that, if avoided, can enable couples to deal with highly volatile issues, such as infidelity, while keeping their marriage intact. More information about Dr. Gottman's research, along with relationship quizzes, books and videos designed to help improve a couple's communication skills, can be found online through The Gottman Institute[2].

If you are reading this because you are considering or facing a divorce, we advise you to invest some time in understanding how your relationship got to this point. Doing so now could actually save your marriage, if that's an option you're looking for. Thinking longer-term, you may be able to avoid repeating the same mistakes in a future relationship.

Second marriages have a higher rate of divorce than first marriages, which may signal that too few of those who get divorced put enough energy into understanding what happened and how to prevent it from happening again. Finding a root cause may take some time and require the help of a counselor or therapist. An outsider can be especially helpful if you have zeroed in on one potential cause and need to broaden your view to reexamine the whole relationship. A therapist can also assist you in dealing with the difficult emotions that may resurface in such a reexamination.

## Divorce and Happiness

Most people assume that a person stuck in a bad marriage has two choices: stay married and be miserable or get a divorce and be happier. If people weren't convinced that divorce would make them happier, fewer marriages would end. Recently though, the conventional wisdom that divorce is a path to happiness has been challenged. One major study found no evidence that, as a group, unhappily married adults who went on to divorce were any happier afterward than unhappily married people who stayed in the marriage. The researchers also found that two-thirds of unhappily married spouses who stayed married reported that their marriages were happy five years later.[3]

Why doesn't divorce typically make adults happier? The authors of the study suggest that while divorce can eliminate some stresses and sources of potential harm, it may create others. The many processes and events set in motion by divorce are difficult for the divorcée to control and are likely to deeply affect his or her emotional well-being. Complicating factors may include the response of one's spouse to divorce; the reactions of children; potential disappointments and aggravation in custody, child support, and visitation orders; new financial or health stresses for one or both parents; and new relationships or marriages.

Many couples who stayed married did so despite extended periods of being unhappy in the marriage, often for quite serious reasons. The marriage turnarounds were grouped into three categories. The most common were couples who stubbornly resisted any temptation to split. In many cases, the sources of their conflict—including financial problems, job reversals, depression, child problems, or even infidelity—faded with the passage of time. A second group actively worked to solve the problems that led to marital unhappiness. The strategies they used ranged from spending more time together to seeking counseling to even threatening divorce. A third group did little to change their marriage but instead found alternative ways to improve their own happiness.

If you are considering divorce, you have to make a personal decision based on the information available to you. By demonstrating how many once-unhappy couples turned things around and regained marital satisfaction, this research highlights the importance of considering the variety of potential long-term outcomes when making major life decisions. Achieving such a long-term view can be difficult if you are presently very unhappy or angry. You may need to take some time or get some counseling to help ensure you do what is right for you, now and in the future.

## The Financial Implications of Divorce

Those considering divorce tend to focus primarily on the emotional issues that have led to their unhappiness. Most people in this position hope they can make this critical decision without regard to the financial implications. Such concentration on what has led to the dissatisfaction is admirable but may actually hinder them from choosing a path that would result in their most positive outcome. To put it bluntly, sometimes it is easier to mend a relationship that was once strong than it is handle the financial difficulties that arise from divorce. If you are considering getting a divorce because you are unhappy with your current situation, you need to seriously consider how your situation will be after the divorce. It's the old saying: "Look before you leap."

Before buying a home, most of us consider how the purchase will affect us in the short term and long term. One short-term consideration would be how we will come up with the required down payment. Thinking longer term, we calculate the savings we will achieve by deducting our interest payments. We consider how much the home might appreciate over the long term. We plan for the types of repairs we might need to make as the home ages.

People generally have beliefs about the financial impact of divorce based on popular notions, which are often inaccurate. Because they are afraid that their spouse would consider contact with a divorce attorney as a sign that divorce is inevitable, most people wait to make contact until divorce really is almost inevitable. It would be better if people considering divorce talked to an attorney earlier in the decision-making process. This way, as they consider divorce, just as when they make less critical decisions, such as whether to buy a house, they would know what the actual financial impact would be. The bulk of the people we see in our law practice do things in reverse. They come to us ready to begin a divorce without having seriously considered the, often life-long, financial implications.

Divorce is tightly connected with finances. In fact, some believe that one cause of the increase in the divorce rate in the 1970s was an increase in married women entering the workplace. Their increased financial independence may have contributed to their willingness to leave their husbands. The changing status of women has continued to shift the financial landscape of divorce. With rights that were more equal came more equal responsibilities; today, while still rare, there are women paying alimony to men.

Negotiations over finances are often the most contentious aspect of divorce. A lot of the conflict arises from the lack of funds that most middle-class couples will experience following divorce. Conflict over finances can be amplified by the emotions divorce stirs up. Often, a spouse who doesn't want the divorce will use financial negotiations as a way to get even with the initiator. This is rarely productive but sometimes does result in an agreement based on the guilt of the initiator. Such agreements are tenuous because the guilt the initiator feels at the time of divorce eventually dissipates, which may lead him or her to reopen the fight.

Most middle-class families spend about as much as they earn, and often a little more. When these families experience divorce, their expenses rise because they must maintain two households. One person leaving a household does little to offset the expense of a new household, because expenses such as mortgage are independent of the number of people in the house. Even though the spouse who is leaving may move into an inexpensive apartment, the second household generally costs at least 40 percent as much as the first.

When you consider the additional expenses incurred by maintaining a second household, it is quite clear that divorce creates a financial hardship. It is common for couples, at the request of their lawyers, to create monthly budgets for their new lives and then to be surprised when their expenses greatly exceed their income. It is perfectly natural for everybody to want to keep the standard of living they had prior to the breakup. In general, men wind up faring better financially in divorce than women. The most commonly cited statistics indicate that, on average, men raise their standard of living by 10 percent while women experience a decline of 27 percent.[4] While we won't argue with the statistics, our experience is that this gap is narrowing and that it's rare for either party to come out a financial winner in divorce.

Since divorce results in increased expenses, those with an already-tight budget need to seriously consider how they will adjust their finances to make ends meet post-divorce. Usually a mix of expense reduction and additional income is required, both of which generally mean painful choices and changes. Expense reduction is sometimes achieved by selling the family home, trading in cars for less expensive models, changing shopping and dining habits, or eliminating private school or summer camp.

Income is typically increased as a parent who has not been working, or has been working part time, returns to full employment. When children are involved, this scenario can create new problems, because the stay-at-home parent may need to be replaced with another caregiver while he or she works. Another, longer term, income-enhancement strategy involves one spouse increasing skills through college or other training. When considered carefully, such training can pay for itself rather quickly, but it is likely to create a short-term financial and time burden. Making plans for career changes or enhancements is difficult when one is going through a divorce, but it may be necessary in order to create a financial plan that meets the goals of both spouses.

Planning budgets that work over the long term is an important part of the divorce process, but the short-term costs of divorce also need to be considered. The costs involved in a noncontentious divorce in which lawyers handle negotiations will usually range between $5,000 and $30,000, depending on where you live and the lawyers you each choose. While you don't pay directly for your spouse's attorney, you do pay indirectly, as the assets or debts you will divide are affected.

# Divorce and Children

Couples with children often face an agonizing choice when considering whether to divorce. They wonder whether they should stay together for the sake of their kids. Will it be better for their kids to have easy access to both parents, even though those parents are often locked in battle? Parents doing their best to raise emotionally healthy children wonder if divorcing creates an example that will be followed by their children in adulthood. These are serious issues. Researchers provide some general guidance, but warn that the effects of divorce on children are not uniform.

The conventional wisdom on divorce has been that whatever is good for the parents will be good for the children. That is, if divorce results in a happier, more optimistic parent, the child will be better off, even if time with the other parent is reduced. Some initial research dealing with the effects of divorce on children supports this position. However, a more recent, larger-scale, longer-term study suggests otherwise. It found that, while the parents' marital unhappiness has a broad negative impact on virtually every dimension of the children's well-being, the parents' divorce has a similar negative impact. Only children in very high-conflict homes were found to benefit from the reduction in conflict that is often associated with divorce. In lower-conflict marriages that end in divorce, which account for approximately two-thirds of divorces, the situation of the children was made much worse following a divorce.[5]

If divorce cannot be seen as an improvement of circumstance for most children in the short term, can these children recover relatively quickly? Again, the most recent research—both in small, qualitative studies and large-scale, long-term studies—indicates that the answer is no. The effects of divorce are long lasting. Even grown children whose parents have re-married since their divorce sometimes wish for their parents to reunite. The children of divorce usually do eventually get past the psychological issues they experience as a result of divorce, but it is not unusual for these children to still be working through these issues into their thirties.

Finally, while it would make sense that children of divorce would be cautious about getting married and, having first-hand knowledge of the pain of divorce, be determined to avoid it, this is not what usually happens. The divorce rate among children of divorce is much higher than that among children raised in intact families. A recent study found that one major reason for this is simply that the children of divorce do not consider marriage to be a lifelong commitment. They never witnessed an example of sustaining a marriage through the difficult periods experienced in almost all families.

## Making the Decision to Divorce

The preceding sections on how divorce affects happiness, finances, and children were not meant to create undue anxiety about your decision. Our job isn't to take a stand on whether you should try to stay married or not. We have come to believe that people considering divorce should be sure that their problems are serious enough that divorce is the preferable path. By providing you with the best information available and making you aware of your options, we are attempting to enable you to come to your own smart decision and find your own path to growing and learning through life's challenges.

As we said at the beginning of this chapter, few people are prepared for divorce before it happens. Now that we have given you some background information to use in creating a realistic expectation of how divorce might affect your life, we certainly understand if you have some hesitation about how to move forward. It's important for those contemplating divorce to realize that it's not the only option available to them.

---

# Marriage Counseling

Marriage counselors certainly wish people would talk to them before they ever contemplate divorce. Even though you and your spouse may have missed that opportunity, a counselor may still be able to help. In this section, we will use the words counseling and therapy interchangeably. In the next section, we will discuss some of the various titles you may run across when looking for counseling.

Marriage counseling is usually a short-term therapy that may, in only a few sessions, help you work out problems in your relationship. Marriage counseling helps couples learn to deal more effectively with problems, and can help prevent small problems from becoming serious. On average, couples work with marital therapists for twelve sessions. There is usually a connection between the relationship problems and the symptoms experienced by one spouse. For example, if you are constantly arguing with your spouse, you will probably also be chronically anxious, angry, or depressed, or all of these things. If you have difficulty controlling your temper, you're likely to have more arguments with your partner. A great thing about marriage counseling is that, when effective, it improves not only the relationship but also a person's physical and mental health.

Sometimes marriage counseling is very similar to individual psychotherapy, though sometimes it is more like mediation, and sometimes it is educational. A combination of approaches can improve the effectiveness of counseling, which therapists are always hoping to do. Some therapists even base their sessions on Dr. John Gottman's principles for a successful marriage, such as building fondness, admiration, and closeness, as a means of altering the behaviors that can later lead to divorce.[6]

Because change can be very hard work, the recommendations provided by a therapist during counseling are likely to create some discomfort in both spouses. In order to give the counseling a serious chance to make the difference you are seeking, both spouses should commit to attending for a specific number of sessions, typically between six and twelve. You should also agree that during the time period in which you are working on improving your relationship, neither of you will do things to harm the marriage, such as moving out, withdrawing or spending large amounts of money, or having relations with a third party.

Therapists have different approaches to their work. About two-thirds of therapists believe that they should remain neutral regarding whether you stay married. They might help you create a sort of cost-benefit analysis about the marriage and whether it should be saved. Others have the mindset that, except where there's abuse and danger, they should try to support the possibility that you can salvage your marriage. This type of therapist will advocate staying together. Of course, they realize that they may be unsuccessful in their efforts, but these therapists view saving the marriage as their goal.

It's our belief that the work of improving and maintaining your relationship with your spouse is a life-long process best accomplished by focusing on your relationship regularly. Although it will require ongoing planning and commitment, this time with your spouse will help you avoid sliding backward and can provide great rewards.

# Finding a Marriage Counselor

There is limited regulation regarding who can call themselves marriage counselors, so it's important to be alert when choosing someone to help you. Many who are trained to work with individuals expand their practices to include marriage counseling, but they may have limited training and experience in the unique skills required to effectively help couples. Marital therapy is the most difficult form of therapy. A therapist whose style when working with individuals is to be empathic and clarifying can be overwhelmed when faced with a couple's conflict. Such a therapist may revert to persuading the couple to work on their issues individually. This approach can lead to failure, because the couple did not come to work on individual problems. Usually one spouse was reluctant to get help together and is likely to be even less willing to go to individual therapy.

Because of the special skills required in counseling couples, you need to make sure you learn of the training and educational background of any counselor you are considering. If the therapist is self-taught or workshop-trained and can't point to significant education in this work, then consider going elsewhere. It's also useful to ask what percentage of the counselor's practice is marital therapy. Be careful if a counselor is mostly focused on individual therapy.

The American Association for Marriage and Family Therapy (AAMFT) is the primary professional association for marriage therapists. Membership in the association requires a minimum of a master's degree and specific graduate training in marriage and family therapy, including supervision by experienced therapists. The AAMFT website includes a therapist-locator service.

While the AAMFT site may represent an easy way to get the names of some therapists, it can also be helpful to ask friends, family members, a religious leader, or, if your company has one, an employee-assistance counselor. The best source of information about professionals, however, is the other professionals. If you know or are seeing a counselor, ask that person for a referral to a marriage counselor. Your own individual therapist has the added advantage of knowing not just the mental health professional community but also your personality and situation, which can help your therapist recommend someone who would be a particularly good fit for you and your spouse.

When considering therapists, remember to ask about their fees, what insurance they accept, and the average length of therapy. While costs are legitimately a part of your decision process, recognize that making a choice because a certain therapist is covered by your insurance plan or promises quick results may be very short sighted. If you believe you may be able to save your marriage, we suggest that you get the best help possible. If you are successful, you will likely save greatly in the long run.

Finally, after you look at a therapist's credentials and experience and consider any recommendations you receive, do two more things. First, trust your instincts. Make sure this is someone you feel comfortable sharing intimate and emotional information with. Second, make sure that your spouse is also comfortable with the choice. If he or she is a reluctant participant, you need to make doubly sure that the counselor is someone you are both comfortable with.

---

# Alternatives to Counseling

Marriage counseling is not the only avenue you can consider if you want to try to stay together. Many alternatives exist, the most popular being weekend retreats that are quite different from counseling. Although it may be hard to believe that one weekend can make much of a difference in a long-troubled relationship, we have had clients who came into our office ready to begin divorce proceedings but then reconciled after attending one of these programs.

One popular weekend program places emphasis on a particular technique of communication between husband and wife. Couples attend in-depth presentations that focus on a specific area of a marriage relationship. They then reflect on and discuss the presentations in private. Although the weekends provide an opportunity to interact with others facing trouble in their marriages, couples do not share any aspect of their marriages with the group. The sponsors, who state up front that the weekends are not a "miracle cure," have designed follow-up sessions to build on the progress made during the weekend.

Many of these weekend programs are faith based but welcome people of all religions. You may want to check with a leader of your spiritual community about a similar program within your faith. One program that is usually led by mental health professionals is Practical Application of Intimate Relationship Skills (PAIRS). The group offers a variety of relationship courses, ranging from one-day sessions to multi-session courses consisting of 120 hours spread over several months.

In an ideal world, couples would take measures such as attending these marriage weekends recreationally. Some couples plan an annual marriage checkup, sometimes involving a restoration vacation, just as they might go to a doctor for a physical checkup. There are even some programs specifically designed for this. Without making a specific plan to nurture your marriage, it's easy to let work, kids, and health issues take priority. Just as with a physical problem, finding a relationship issue early and dealing with it can avoid a lot of pain in the long run.

# Trial Separation

Sometimes couples facing serious marital discord consider separating on a trial basis. Trial separations can give each spouse, particularly the one who wants the divorce, a chance to experience how life might be after divorce. The separation can also be used to reduce the intensity of conflict between the spouses so they can work with a counselor and then decide whether to reconcile or divorce.

Trial separation seems like a reasonable idea in theory, but in practice, we rarely see couples get back together after they separate. It's possible that this approach works better than we think, because people may separate and reconcile without ever seeing a lawyer. We don't think that's the case, though, because trial separation has two significant downsides. First, one party in the separation may enjoy being alone during the short time the separation lasts. The conflict reduction may overpower any sense of loneliness that comes with time. Second, while couples who are having trouble face great challenges improving their relationship while living together, if they separate, the work can become even harder. Once separated, you might only see your spouse at counseling. That doesn't allow you to apply the lessons learned at counseling in between the sessions. It becomes difficult, even impossible, to learn a new way of successfully interacting on a daily basis.

Sometimes lawyers will suggest trial separation as a strategy to get a reluctant spouse to move forward with the divorce process. The leaving spouse may suggest that the separation is only a trial separation when this is not that spouse's true intent. We have mixed feelings about this practice. Trial separation may be a less harsh way to introduce divorce to a spouse having difficulty handling the full impact of divorce at one time. Even so, we generally believe that being honest at the beginning of the divorce is important in maintaining the credibility that will be required during the negotiations to come.

If you do begin a trial separation, try to come to an agreement with your spouse beforehand. Generally, if you both agree to the separation, you will not be getting into complicated legal territory. Regardless, you need to consider, and ideally put in writing, what property and cars will go with the person who is leaving, whom the children will stay with and how will they be cared for, and how bills will be paid. Beyond these issues make sure you are clear about access to the marital home. Will a knock before entry be sufficient? What if nobody is home? Finally, try to agree on how you will communicate the separation to children and friends.

A trial separation generally refers to a situation in which both spouses agree to the separation. If you and your spouse are not in agreement and you wish to leave, you should consult an attorney for help in ensuring that your rights are protected.

# Notes

[1]Xenia P. Montenegro, PhD., "The Divorce Experience: A Study of Divorce at Midlife and Beyond," *AARP The Magazine* (May 2004). http://assets.aarp.org/rgcenter/general/divorce.pdf.

[2] John Mordechai Gottman and Nan Silver, *Why Marriages Succeed or Fail and How You Can Make Yours Last* (New York: Simon & Schuster, 1995). http://www.gottman.com/shop/why-marriages-succeed-or-fail/.

[3] Linda J. Waite, "Does Divorce Make People Happy?: Findings from a Study of Unhappy Marriages," *Institute for American Values* (2002). http://americanvalues.org/search/item.php?id=13.

[4] Richard R. Peterson, "A Re-Evaluation of the Economic Consequences of Divorce," *American Sociological Review* 61 no. 3 (1996): 528. http://www.jeremyfreese.com/docs/Peterson-Weitzman-Peterson - FullASRDebate.pdf.

[5] Susan M. Jekielek, "Parental Conflict, Marital Disruption and Children's Emotional Well-Being," *Social Forces* 76, no. 3 (1998): 905. http://sf.oxfordjournals.org/content/76/3/905.full.pdf.

[6] John M. Gottman and Nan Silver, *The Seven Principles for Making Marriage Work* (Toronto: Random House, 1999).

# An Overview of Divorce

Divorce is a transition people move through, taking between several months and several years. During this time, you must accomplish a number of practical tasks while at the same time dealing with what are likely to be intense emotions. This chapter provides an overview of the divorce process. Although most of the topics we cover will get much more attention in later chapters, it's useful to first get this overall view. With this context, you will be able to consider how the information and advice we provide in future chapters fits into your divorce as a whole.

## Defining Your Goals

The first step of your divorce should be considering your goals. Even if divorce is not your choice, you need to think past the immediate pain or anger you may be feeling to help yourself make the best of the situation. Most often, one spouse initiates divorce and the other feels some degree of surprise and shock. Because the initiator decides when to tell the other spouse about the decision, he or she may have developed a plan for life after the divorce. Noninitiating spouses can be at a temporary disadvantage, because they usually come into the process unprepared, sometimes even blindsided. They run the risk of going through the divorce in survival mode, able to focus only on getting through the day or over the next hurdle. They may have no concept of how life will be, or how they want it to be, after divorce.

Going through divorce in survival mode is unlikely to allow you to achieve your best possible outcome or learn much from your experience. Whether you are the person making the decision or have been surprised

23

by your spouse's decision, you should try to create a realistic picture of your life after divorce. This may be difficult or impossible if you are experiencing depression. If that's the case, you may need to consider getting some individual therapy, if you aren't already.

If you are able to create a positive picture of life after divorce, use that to guide you as you move through this transition. As you learn more about the divorce process, you will continually adjust your mental picture to align it with reality. For instance, after you begin to understand your post-divorce finances, you may conclude that you will have to move to a smaller house or change jobs. Regardless, a focus on where you are going will help you maintain control of your situation.

Divorce involves a series of decisions. You are even going to need to decide *how* you and your spouse will make major decisions. Rather than making each decision independently, try to be proactive and keep your long-term goals in mind to guide you in your decision making; this will make the process easier for you and help you feel in control rather than powerless.

As you envision your life after divorce, ask yourself:

- What type of relationship do you want to have with your former spouse? The way you handle the divorce will affect your future relationship.
- What roles do you want each of you to play in the lives of your children?
- Will you be reentering the workforce?
- Will you be changing to a career that requires more college or professional training?

Everyone has had the experience of making a decision they later regret. Sometimes it's impossible to know how things will turn out. But sometimes we realize that if we had just done a little more planning beforehand, we might have chosen differently and perhaps achieved better results. This is your time to do that work—to create a vision for the next stage of your life and then make decisions that will help you turn that vision into a reality.

It can be extremely difficult to do long-term planning amid the pain of divorce. You may need to get assistance from a supportive friend or even a therapist as you think through what you need and want for the future. Do what you can to get this long-range perspective. Those who fail to do the planning and are unable to focus on the long term usually have regrets. For instance, if you focus too much on the immediate gratification of getting back at your spouse, you may unwittingly undermine your long-term needs for emotional stability and financial security. If you keep a cool head and plan your future life with carefully thought-out goals, you will be creating the kind of life that you want and deserve for yourself, to the greatest extent you can.

## Choosing a Process

Some divorces go smoothly. The spouses are able to maintain civility, negotiate an agreement covering the major issues of divorce, cooperate in raising their children, and even remain friends. Other divorces rival the worst cases you may have seen in TV or movies—the divorce becomes a war, with each side attacking the other in any way possible. Two people who must have loved each other at some point in the past can act in ways that were completely foreign to them prior to the divorce. Sometimes the personalities of the players make things so ugly, but just as often, it's the actual process they're going through that brings out the worst in everyone. It's essential to understand the steps involved in getting divorced so that you can choose the process that causes the *least* amount of misery in your life.

From a legal and financial perspective, divorce involves creating an agreement between you and your spouse about how you will divide your property, provide or receive financial support, care for your children, and pay for the children's needs. Although different states refer to the agreement by different names (including marital settlement agreement, property settlement agreement, and separation agreement), we will refer to it as a divorce agreement. In an ideal world, you and your spouse would sit down together and create your own agreement. You would need to make sure you were aware of your rights and responsibilities, but you would be in control of the decisions. At the opposite extreme, you fail to reach an agreement and a judge creates one for you in the form of a court order.

It is rare for couples to negotiate their divorce agreement themselves without legal assistance. It is even more rare for judges to make all the decisions. In fact, less than 1 percent of divorces end up in court. Between these extremes are a range of options we refer to as the *Spectrum of Control*, which includes:

- Self-Help
- Collaborative Law
- Mediation
- Lawyer-Led Negotiation
- Arbitration
- Litigation

We will go into more detail about each option later in the book; for now, we just want to introduce the concepts. This will allow you to begin considering if, when, and how you want to involve a lawyer in your divorce.

*Self-help divorce* is what we call the process used by couples who negotiate directly, without the help of divorce professionals such as lawyers or mediators. This process keeps you highly involved in the negotiation of your divorce agreement. Unless your spouse is very controlling, or you are unable to express and negotiate for what you want, working together to define each aspect of the agreement lets you maintain a high degree of control.

While self-help divorce lets you maintain control, without professional advice, you run the risk of inadvertently giving up your rights. Divorce laws are complicated; it is rare that both spouses have the time, energy, and desire to learn them to the degree necessary to preserve their rights. In all but the simplest cases, we recommend that each party retain the services of a lawyer to at least advise them of their rights and review their agreement before they sign it. Using a lawyer does not mean that you are heading to court, but as we will discuss later, you do need to be careful about the lawyer you select. Lawyers often rely on the threat of going to court to give them leverage in negotiations. Such threats can escalate disagreements into wars, which are often not in your best interest.

The relatively new *collaborative law* process is one way to get the benefits of an attorney without the threat-laden, adversarial approach attorneys have been trained for (and sometimes have difficulty avoiding). Collaborative divorce is a set of voluntary ground rules entered into by the attorneys hired by you and your spouse. While the details vary from lawyer to lawyer, the central idea is that the parties hire lawyers who agree in advance not to take the case to trial. If your case cannot be settled and you decide to litigate, you both have to hire new attorneys.

If you are someone who says, "We are only going to hire lawyers if we can't work it out and it gets really ugly," then collaborative divorce is probably for you. Collaborative divorce lawyers help you make good decisions about financial issues. For example, they advise you about the hidden pitfalls of the tax code and the intricate rules imposed by the US Department of Labor and Internal Revenue Service governing retirement plans. They make sure you don't make document-drafting mistakes that cost both parties in ways they didn't expect. Collaborative divorce lawyers make sure you understand the law, your rights, your obligations, and the legal effects of your decisions.

The next step along the Spectrum of Control is *mediation*. Mediation allows you and your spouse to reach a fair settlement with the help of a third, neutral party called a mediator. Mediators, who can be lawyers, mental health professionals, clergy members, or other professionals trained in alternative dispute resolution techniques, help you and your spouse identify and resolve issues. The most important thing to understand is that mediators *cannot* give either of you legal advice—a mediator is not a substitute for your own lawyer. The mediator's role is to help you and your spouse communicate and reach agreement, while your lawyer's role is to make sure your legal rights are protected.

*Lawyer-led negotiation* is the most common process used for creating a divorce agreement when lawyers are involved. This approach is often selected when the degree of animosity between the spouses keeps them from being able to work together productively in the same room, as is required by the collaborative law and mediation processes. Although in lawyer-led negotiation you still decide whether the terms of the agreement are acceptable to you, your lawyer works with your spouse's lawyer to create the agreement.

During negotiations, your lawyer should share with you any written correspondence sent to or received from the other lawyer. However, there is likely to be a fair amount of verbal communication between the lawyers. Your lawyer will likely discuss the content of these conversations with you, but here you get into playing the old game of telephone, where interpretation begins to play a significant role. You generally are trying to understand what is important to your spouse so you can consider where you are willing to bend in order to get what is important to you. Your spouse's words are filtered by his or her attorney and then by your attorney. Of course, the same is happening in reverse. The attorneys have their own biases, which certainly get added to the mix. In the end, while this process often makes sense, the risk of miscommunication can really slow the process down.

*Arbitration* and *litigation* are the processes that provide you with the least control over your divorce. These nearly equivalent processes are used when negotiations break down. In both arbitration and litigation, you place the decisions regarding your divorce in the hands of a third party.

When you choose to arbitrate, you and your spouse split the fee for an arbitrator (rather than the state paying for the judge). Arbitrators, unlike mediators, act as judges. They are professionals trained to hear testimony, take evidence, and issue actual decisions for the couple. When divorcing partners decide to arbitrate their case, all parties must first sign an arbitration agreement. This document gives the arbitrator decision-making authority, narrows the issues to be resolved, and defines whether the arbitrated award will be binding and thus become a court order.

As in mediation, you and your spouse usually both hire attorneys to help with the arbitration process, so that you are both advised and represented by experienced divorce lawyers. During arbitration there is an actual "hearing," similar to a court hearing, but in a less formal setting. There are opening statements, presentations of the evidence, cross-examination, and closing arguments. As in a court trial, you have little control over the outcome.

We will consider arbitration and litigation in more detail in future chapters. Neither option is one we recommend you choose without first at least trying to reach agreement by means of a less adversarial process. Not only do you have the least control over your divorce with arbitration and litigation but they are also the most expensive processes because of the extensive preparation work that must be done before arbitration or a court trial. If you wish to or, because of children, need to be on good terms with your spouse after the divorce, having your agreement dictated by a third party is not the most amicable way to move into the next phase of your relationship.

---

# Telling Your Spouse

Marriages do not die suddenly. It is most common for one spouse to consider divorce, possibly talk to a lawyer, and then make a final decision before the other spouse. The initiator has choices regarding how to tell the other spouse of the decision. The way you handle telling your spouse what you've decided can have a tremendous effect on the whether your divorce process goes smoothly.

In one particularly ugly but all too common scenario, one spouse has committed adultery and the other spouse (either intentionally or unintentionally) finds out. Of course, when this happens, the divorce process begins with the noninitiator being surprised and angry. Although it is usually the case that both parties played a role in the disintegration of the marriage, ending a marriage this way is likely to make the noninitiator feel like a victim who has been wronged and is due some form of compensation. If he or she does assume the victim role, it is almost certain that negotiations will fail. The initiator may, at first, attempt to appease the spouse's demands but will likely eventually become angry and fight back, causing things to escalate rather than move toward settlement. All in all, it's a bad situation that just keeps getting worse.

Ideally, you and your spouse will both agree that your marriage should end. If you can reach a mutual decision, your chances of settling the major issues outside of court are greatly increased. Although it is most comfortable to get everything in order before telling your spouse that the marriage is over, it is really best to involve your spouse as soon as possible in order to increase the likelihood that the decision will be mutual.

When talking to your spouse about your feelings or your decision, you will want to calmly review the problems in your marriage that make you feel that divorce is necessary. If you have already taken actions to head off divorce, review those efforts with your spouse. Let him or her know why you feel things are not working out.

To avoid escalating the conversation into a fight, you will want to avoid blaming your spouse. A traditional approach to communicating about a problem without accusing the other person of being the cause is to use "'I' statements." With these, you refer to how something that is happening makes you feel, such as by saying, "I feel disappointed that we don't spend evenings together like we used to." This is a much softer way to communicate this thought than the more blameful, "You never come home on time and you never call to warn me." You may be angry in the short term, but your long-term interests will be best served by keeping this conversation from exploding.

Shock, denial, and anger are all feelings that are experienced by a noninitiator during the initial upheaval of a divorce they were not expecting. These emotions can make your first conversations very difficult. The first time you broach the issue will probably be the most difficult. If your spouse is overwhelmed, try taking a break to let calmer heads prevail before continuing the conversation. You may find that you need to talk to your spouse about your intention to divorce several times before he or she begins to understand and accept that you are serious and have made up your mind.

# Telling Your Children

Most young children of divorce wake up one day to find that one parent has left the home. This naturally leads to fear that the other parent might be gone one day as well. While it's the relationship with your spouse that is the cause of your divorce, your actions will have a serious effect on your children. Jointly planning the way you tell your children about what is happening is one of the most important things you can do to help your children successfully navigate this critical turning point in their lives.

It is difficult for us to offer blanket advice about talking with children, because children change so much as they progress along the developmental ladder. One book we think deals with this subject in an excellent way is *What About the Kids?: Raising Your Children Before, During, and After Divorce* by Judith S. Wallerstein and Sandra Blakeslee. The book stands out because it details what is important to children at each developmental stage. Children will feel that the divorce threatens their way of life, which it very well might, and the more you can understand how they interpret the world, the better you will be at reassuring them that things will be all right.

The timing of telling your children is critical. You definitely want to avoid waiting until just before, or even after, one of you has left the home. Children need time to prepare. The amount of time required for this preparation varies depending on the child's age. Wallerstein recommends telling children younger than five just a day or two before you separate, school-age children a few days to a week ahead, and adolescents at least two weeks before. If your spouse leaves suddenly, you obviously won't have an opportunity to prepare the children. In this case, Wallerstein advises that you "apologize to your children and admit candidly that you just learned of it, that you want to keep them informed, and that had you known in advance, you would have told them." [7]

While waiting until your marriage has already broken up to tell children can be harmful, you can create other problems if you tell them things are definite before they really are. Your children will want you to reunite. If you tell them you are divorcing and then you get back together and then you split up again, they will have difficulty sorting things out.

Children of divorce report that the memory of the day their parents announced their divorce stays with them for many years. Wallerstein recommends you plan two "family meetings" to discuss the divorce. The first meeting is a chance to tell them what you are doing without going into excessive detail. The second meeting gives you a chance to add the things you may have realized you left out of the first discussion. The second meeting also allows you to ask your kids what they remember from the first conversation. You may get a surprising response, particularly from younger kids, because they may have heard what they wanted to hear or expanded on what they heard. You will want to gently remind them of the discussion and reinforce things to help them grasp what is happening. The second meeting makes things concrete. This is when you should add the details of the children's schedule, including when they will see each parent and how anything affecting their lives will change.

When you talk to your children, remember to tell them that you and your spouse loved each other when you got married and never expected to divorce. Having this understanding will help protect their self-esteem and let them know that they came from a loving family. If it's true, remind them of how you wanted them and the joy you both felt when they were born. Then you can begin to tell them what has happened to cause you, your spouse, or both of you to feel that divorce is necessary. Of course, you will need to tailor your talk to the developmental needs of the children.

Wallerstein warns against the "real estate approach," in which you say simply that you will live here and your spouse will live elsewhere but give no explanation. Children need some explanation. She says that the simple statement that you are "different people" is insufficient. If one parent feels the need for more involvement than a spouse who is happiest working long hours can offer, you can tell the children that you have different ideas about how you want to live and that neither of you would be happy if you had to change. If one parent has a substance abuse problem, let the children know (if you can do so truthfully) that he or she tried to resolve it but couldn't, and that staying together would not allow for the happy household you want for them.

The problem in your marriage may be difficult to explain in terms children will understand and in a way that is not blameful. Wallerstein advises to:

> Be gentle. Telling the truth does not mean that you should depre-cate or scapegoat each other. Because you and your spouse cannot make your marriage work, and things between you can only get worse, say you've decided to divorce for everyone's sake. You don't want your children to grow up with the wrong view of what marriage is. You don't want to live a lie or mislead them into thinking that your failing marriage is the best that marriage provides. It isn't.[8]

In the magazine *Families in Transition*, child psychologist Matt Mendell provides the following guidelines for minimizing the harmful impact of telling your children about divorce:

- Children should not be told until the decision is definite.
- Telling is not a one-time thing: all important messages need to be repeated.
- Ideally, parents should tell the children together.
- Telling should be done without blaming or criticizing either parent. (Think of this as your first big step in the ongoing task of supportive coparenting.)
- Tell the facts, but without unnecessary or age-inappropriate detail.
- Let the children know that this is something that you've thought about a lot, talked about, and planned (and talked to a therapist or a minister about...). Children need to know that this was not an impulsive or capricious decision, and that it is final.
- Tell them, repeatedly, that Mommy will always be their mommy or Daddy will always be their daddy, and that both of you will always love them.
- Tell them that the decision to get a divorce was entirely be-cause of problems between you and your spouse and had

33

nothing at all to do with them. That is, make very clear to them that they did not do anything to cause the divorce. (This is an especially big issue with young children who, because of their age-appropriate self-centeredness, often assume they must have done something to bring about these events.)

- Emphasize to them that they will continue to see both parents, even though it will be in two different homes now.

- Empathize with their feelings. Provide opportunities for them to talk about their feelings, repeatedly—with each parent and with a therapist, counselor, or minister. Acknowledge to them that it is entirely natural and understandable that they feel angry, sad, scared, confused, and whatever other feelings they may have.

Pay particular attention to the advice to make it clear that the divorce is not your children's fault. They may decide that any recent discipline issue you have had with them has led to the divorce. They might attempt to correct their behavior in hopes of making the divorce go away. Make it very clear that children do not cause divorce and that what causes divorce has to do with parents.

We suggest you review these guidelines together and, if possible, practice what you will say together. Your goal isn't to create an act that fails to represent how upset you are about the divorce. On the contrary, you want your children to understand the gravity of the situation. If you work together on what you say, you will help to ensure the communication is as clear as possible.

## Separating

Earlier, we discussed the concept of trial separation, an approach that some people use in an effort to save their marriage. Here, we deal with the for-real separation period that generally precedes a divorce. Separating from your spouse is a major step that affects your entire family, legally, financially, and emotionally. From a legal and financial perspective, the fact that you or your spouse have choices regarding who will leave, and when, may be closely tied to the overall negotiations of your divorce agreement. While you may have found that discussing divorce with your spouse and children is difficult, you may experience even more intense emotions as you or your spouse prepares to leave. The leaving can make something that seemed abstract suddenly become very real.

People separate at different points in the divorce process and with different degrees of preparation. Some people separate in the midst of a fight and make no arrangements for how they will live their lives during the separation. The partners may not have yet discussed divorce with each other or their children. Others work with lawyers and negotiate a complete separation agreement prior to one or both of them leaving the marital home. Still others separate at a time when one of them is dealing with the initial emotional upheaval of the divorce and is unable to make long-term decisions. In this situation, the couple may use lawyers or a mediator or both to create a temporary agreement that addresses how children and finances will be handled during the separation. Once a limited agreement is in place, the couple can take some time to emotionally prepare for the negotiation of a more comprehensive and permanent agreement.

While much of what you need to do to get divorced is the same nationwide, there are a few issues that are handled quite differently from state to state. Separation is one of these. Whether or not you intend to use a family law attorney during the negotiation of your divorce agreement, we highly recommend that you consult with a lawyer prior to separating. This is especially true if you have children or own your home. You will want to understand *your* state's laws and get some advice regarding how leaving the home might affect you as you negotiate your divorce agreement.

When you talk to a lawyer about separation in your state, you should make sure you get answers to at least the following questions:

- Is separation required prior to getting a divorce?
- Will I need a separation agreement to get a divorce?
- What is considered separation? Can we just live in separate rooms?
- Will separating affect my custody rights?

- Will separating affect my responsibility to pay or receive alimony?
- How do I need to document alimony payments in order to ensure they are tax deductible?

We cannot cover each state's laws relating to separation, but we will address some common issues you will face in thinking about separation, regardless of the state in which you are divorcing.

In general, a formal "legal separation," in which a court filing or order is involved, is not necessary. Some states require that you separate from your spouse for a period of up to a year before finalizing your divorce. However, with the notable exception of New York, it is usually not necessary to complete a court filing or specific agreement with your spouse to make the separation valid. You may just need to stop living together. Even where an agreement is not required, having an agreement that clearly states your rights and obligations during the separation is advisable.

Before you even consider when you should move out and the type of agreement you will want to have in place, you may be concerned about whether it is financially feasible for you to maintain a separate residence. However, we have to point out, at this juncture, one really important exception to our advice to move slowly: *if you are in danger, you should leave, regardless.* See our chapter on domestic violence for further information. If you are experiencing, or expect to experience, a great deal of stress staying with your spouse after your decision to divorce but feel that you cannot afford to leave, this may be a time to make use of savings or credit or even borrow from relatives or friends to get away from the situation. Sometimes even someone who is likely to receive property or support when the divorce is complete is unable to pay for a separate residence because the other spouse has blocked access to property or accounts. In these situations, the law usually provides a way to go to court and get a portion of what you are likely to receive from your divorce in advance, so that you can meet your needs until the divorce is finalized. If you want to leave but are truly unable to do so, you will want to arrange your household so that you and your spouse are as separate as possible.

Your decision about who moves out, and when, may be the first step in negotiating the terms of your divorce agreement. If you are working with an attorney prior to separation, you are likely to be advised to consider how moving out affects your bargaining position in your divorce negotiations. Consider the case where, after hearing of the husband's decision to divorce, his spouse wants him to leave the house. If the husband is able to handle the stress of living with his eventual ex during negotiations, we may advise him to stay in order to provide an incentive for his spouse to move the negotiations forward quickly. By staying, it is possible that he will be able to get concessions in his divorce agreement that he otherwise would not have received.

It may seem easiest to leave the house, so you can get moving on with your new life. But if you are in the position of being asked to leave, you need to consider how your new life will be affected by having incomplete divorce negotiations hanging over your head for several months or even a year or more. Staying in the house under these circumstances is definitely a hardball tactic for which we, as lawyers, take some heat. However, we have seen the less acute but longer-term effects of living in limbo. In those cases, a spouse who moved out may be unable to buy a new house because he or she is uncertain about what the post-divorce financial situation will be. Even worse can be living for a lengthy period with uncertainty about how much time you will be able to spend with your children.

You might consider resolution of some divorce issues enticement enough for you to leave. However, before you make that decision, you need to seriously consider how long it may take to resolve the remaining issues. We have seen issues that people thought were settled get put back into the negotiations when they worked to finalize partial or temporary arrangements from before or during separation. We will discuss negotiating strategy in more detail later in the book. For now, you should know that, when negotiating, it is best if you can resolve all issues at once rather than working piecemeal. This approach is more likely to get you what is most important to you and save you money, which can be wasted if negotiations are drawn out.

The hardball approach is not for everyone. Living together may help keep the pressure on to resolve the divorce negotiations quickly, but you have to consider the price. Continuing to live together is likely to stifle the adjustment process for you and your spouse. If you are spending your time fighting, you are unable to focus on preparing for your life after divorce. While your strategy may be to get your spouse to make concessions in exchange for you moving out, there is a chance of this backfiring if, in frustration, your spouse abandons negotiations in favor of court. You will need to consider the effects on your children as well. Having both of you in the house can be confusing and can fuel their hopes that you will reconcile. While we sometimes recommend that spouses stay in the home, you will have to consider the goals of your divorce, what is happening in your house, and whether the negotiating advantage is worth it to you.

Although it may be obvious, it is worth stating that if your spouse is threatening to leave, there is not a whole lot, from a legal and financial perspective, you can do. Being the first to go may not substantially hurt anyone's position, but it also won't enhance it, so you don't really need to push for the creation of an agreement before he or she leaves. If your spouse later tries to return against your wishes, you may be able to take legal action to prevent this from happening.

If you are in the unfortunate situation of wishing your spouse would leave, but it doesn't look like that's going to happen anytime soon, consider these excellent tips from Diana Mercer and Marsha Kline Pruett in their book, *Your Divorce Advisor:*

- Concentrate on keeping relations as peaceful as possible, even if that means ignoring hurtful comments or doing more than your share of the work around the house
- Concentrate on the positive: you are saving money, you have backup help with the house and children, you can take more time to think about what you'd like from the end of the process without having to worry about living arrangements in the short term
- Protect your personal space and privacy, and respect your spouse's personal space and privacy

- Begin to implement separation behaviors: sleep in separate bedrooms, do not engage in sexual activity
- Agree upon what to tell family and friends so that there is no misunderstanding about what the living arrangement signifies

If you are unable to negotiate a comprehensive separation agreement before leaving the home, you can take other steps to safeguard your assets during the period that you and your spouse are negotiating (or litigating) the divorce issues. One of these steps is to take possession of certain assets during separation, especially those assets you wish to use—such as furniture and vehicles—and those assets that might be liquidated by your spouse, including precious gems and stones, collectibles, cash, and bearer bonds.

In some situations, leaving the house may be considered abandonment and may affect findings of fault, which we will discuss later. If you end up in court, the fact that you left may be a factor in the judge's decision. You can usually avoid any negative implications if, before you leave, you and your spouse sign an agreement stating that one of you will move out and that the move is not abandonment or desertion. The agreement may also provide for the possibility that the one who moved out can move back with a specified notice.

Generally, moving out does not jeopardize your financial claim to your house. However, moving out *is* likely to result in you losing access to the house and any property you left behind. Your spouse may change the locks. You may then spend a great deal of time negotiating about which possessions are yours and whether you can have the use of them during the divorce negotiations. You will inevitably leave behind property that will become part of your divorce negotiations. Once you are away from the house, it may become difficult to recall all of these items, especially if they were primarily cared for by your spouse. For instance, many husbands are not very aware of the china and silver they received as wedding gifts and have added to over time. Before moving out, you should try to make an inventory of the items in the house. You might use photos or videos to speed this process and also provide a record of the condition of those items at the time you left.

In our chapter "Divorce and Finances," we will discuss other protective measures you might consider, ranging from closing joint accounts to filing an injunction. In general, unless you are already in a combative mode, these steps should be taken after consulting your spouse. Cutting off access to funds or assets without such a consultation is almost certain to hurt your chances of reaching a settlement quickly.

Couples with children need to have a parenting plan in place during their separation. If you are moving away from the children and expect to later have a large share of the time with them, then you will need to remain an active, involved parent during the separation. If you cannot agree to a plan and one spouse is unsatisfied with how things are going, then you may need to resort to the courts for a temporary custody order. Although your state's laws may indicate that such orders should not affect any permanent custody determinations, if a child is later adjusting to a particular custodial situation, a judge may be unlikely to change things.

Finally, if you do end up negotiating or being presented with an agreement that is intended to be in effect only during your separation period, be careful. You need to avoid the temptation to view such an agreement as temporary; this is because once you agree to something in a separation, it may be considered as a final resolution of that issue in your divorce. You can avoid this outcome by making sure that the agreement indicates that you are not bound to the separation agreement terms in your final divorce agreement.

## Preparing Your Financial Information

At some point in the process of getting your divorce, you will need to collect and understand your financial information in order to negotiate your divorce agreement. In most marriages, one spouse handles the bulk of the financial management. If you are that person, you will have a good idea of where to find all of the information you need. On the other hand, if your spouse handles the finances, you will need to consider how you will most effectively determine the full state of your finances. Often you will need to start copying documents, with or without your spouse's knowledge, prior to separation in order to obtain the full picture. Those documents will need to be stored in a safe place, usually outside of your residence. They should be treated as very valuable, as they may become critical to you if your divorce grows contentious.

Divorce involves dividing assets and may involve the determination of spousal maintenance (alimony) or child support or both, these elements based on your income. You may have assets that are quite easy to identify: house, cars, jewelry, retirement account, etc. If you and your spouse work for others on standard compensation plans, your income will be fairly easy to determine as well. Complexity arises if you have had funds invested in less visible assets, such as property, investment accounts, or businesses that you may not have your name on. We have had cases where spouses who travel frequently have put money in bank accounts in countries that provide a degree of privacy that can make the funds hard to track. A more common issue arises in determining the income of self-employed people or commissioned employees.

Aside from knowing your assets and debts as well as your income, you will need to understand your cash flow. That is, you will need to know what it costs to maintain your current standard of living. In most cases, your standard of living will need to decrease somewhat after the divorce, but as you negotiate spousal maintenance and child support, you need to understand the degree to which you will be affected. If a judge becomes involved in these matters, he will likely take into account your current standard of living.

Because finances are so integral to divorce, we dedicate an entire chapter to the topic. For now, recognize that if you have not been active in managing the finances of your family, you need to begin paying attention and learning so that you can be confident that the information on which you base your divorce negotiations is accurate and complete.

## Getting Emotionally Ready for Negotiations

Divorce is about tangible things such as money and property, but there is a major emotional component as well. You are likely experience a variety of intense emotions as you proceed through each of the steps of divorce we are describing. What we want you to begin to think about now is the necessity of giving yourself and your spouse *time* to reach what we call "emotional readiness" for negotiations.

From an emotional perspective, the initial period of divorce is the most difficult. This is especially true for those who did not initiate the divorce, who are often surprised by their spouse's decision. The spouse who made the decision has usually emotionally detached from the marriage before announcing the plans to separate. The departing spouse may want to complete the divorce as quickly as possible. If this is your position, you might make an initial attempt at negotiating; however, you may be best served by giving your spouse time to grieve for the loss of the relationship he or she has counted on for stability.

Pushing for negotiations before both spouses are ready, which may take months, can result in the process becoming combative. If you are being asked to negotiate early in the process, you may feel a powerful need to punish your spouse for what he or she has done. If you really think about your urge to retaliate, though, you may realize that you will hurt yourself more by holding onto hostile feelings. Playing out your anger at or disappointment with your spouse will almost surely reduce the chances for an amicable, cooperative settlement. Worse, a flaring of tensions could precipitate a court battle that leaves you emotionally scarred and financially ruined.

We realize, though, that recognizing what is good for you and acting on that knowledge are two very different things. If you are unable to control the urge for punitive negotiations, or you see that your spouse wants to get even with you in some way, you will want to slow things down. More time, and possibly counseling, will be required before everyone has reached the emotional readiness for good negotiations to occur. Remember, one of the goals here is to come out on the other side of your divorce a stronger, healthier person.

# The Major Decisions of Divorce

Up to this point we have discussed "divorce negotiations" but have not written much about the specific issues you will be negotiating. There are four major issues in divorce: property division, alimony, child custody, and child support. If you don't have children, or they are adults, you will have less work to do. Because these are the major issues of divorce, each receives complete attention in its own chapter later in the book; at this juncture, we would like to clarify what each issue involves and give you some initial thoughts to consider.

Everyone realizes that getting divorced involves dividing up property, but not many people know exactly what property is included and excluded from the distribution or whether the division is fifty-fifty or some other ratio. For most people, the process of *property distribution* during divorce is fairly simple. Unless you or your spouse owns a business or other asset that is difficult to value, you can avoid most of the complexity involved in dividing your property.

The first step of property distribution involves identifying all of your assets and debts. This relates back to the step above, in which we told you about the need to prepare your financial information. On top of the mortgage and bank and retirement accounts, which you might have documented by gathering recent statements, property division also involves things such as furniture, silver and china, cars, boats, and tools. Ideally, you and your spouse will be able to decide who gets all of these items without the need for a judge. As usual though, consideration of what a judge might do can help keep the negotiations within reasonable bounds.

State laws provide for one of two major approaches to dividing your property: community property or equitable distribution. In states using the *community property* approach, items considered marital property are divided equally. It is a simple system but does not take into account the contributions made by either spouse to the pool of marital property, so it can produce what some consider unfair results. Arizona, California, Idaho, Louisiana, Nevada, New Mexico, Texas, Washington, Wisconsin, and Mississippi (modified) are community-property states.

*Equitable distribution* is the other approach to property distribution. In this more modern system, the property is divided in a way that is intended to be fair. That means it may not be an equal distribution. When a judge is involved, he or she is generally guided by state laws as to the factors taken into consideration when making the determination of what is equitable. These factors are likely to include your standard of living, the amount you contributed to the marriage (potentially including domestic work that allowed a spouse to prosper), and how long you were married. Although judges are given the discretion to make unequal distributions, most cases result in equal splits, even in states using the equitable distribution system.

States vary in what they consider *marital property*. Some states consider all property part of what is to be divided. Most have a concept of *exempt property*. This is generally property you brought into the marriage or inherited. Exempt property may include gifts given directly to you as opposed to the both of you. The challenge here, especially in long marriages, becomes documenting that the property has not become *comingled* with the marital property. Comingling occurs when, for instance, an item you received in an inheritance is sold and the funds received are then combined with marital funds to purchase another item. This newly purchased item is marital property, and is therefore subject to the division process.

A major challenge in the property division process is agreeing on the value of your assets. Generally, the person who wants to keep an item attempts to assign it a lower value. Discrepancies can also occur when people fail to take into account that items should be valued at fair-market value, which is usually far less than what they were bought for, even though they may not be very old.

The next major issue of divorce is *alimony*, which may also be referred to as spousal support or spousal maintenance. Of the divorce issues, alimony is the one with the most variation among the states. However, once again, the concepts and considerations are similar. Alimony is the payment of money by one spouse to the other after a couple is divorced. A temporary arrangement or court order may also result in alimony payments while a couple is separated prior to the divorce becoming final.

Alimony has changed dramatically over the past few decades. The primary driver of the change has been the changing role of women in the workplace. Because prior to the 1970s there were few well-paying jobs available for women, women were not expected to ever be able to earn enough after divorce to meet their needs. Husbands generally agreed, or were ordered, to pay monthly payments to an ex-wife until she remarried or the husband died.

These days, permanent alimony is much more rare, primarily occurring when the partners are wealthy or have had a lengthy marriage. In its place, temporary, or rehabilitative, alimony provides payments for a specified length of time. The general expectation now is that the spouse who receives alimony payments (which occasionally is now the husband) will do so for, at most, a fixed period of time. The underlying concept is that a spouse who had not been working or was working at a reduced level should, in most cases, be able to support him- or herself after some period of training or experience. This assumption is reasonable in some cases, but when a spouse has stayed home for a lengthy period, it may be difficult, or even impossible, for that spouse to achieve anything near the salary level he or she might have earned with uninterrupted work.

Because alimony directly affects the standard of living of each spouse, the negotiations can be extremely contentious. The appearance of a discrepancy between the relative standards of living of the two spouses can create resentment. If you are unable to come to agreement and a judge has to decide on the amount and duration of alimony, be aware that judges often have broad discretion and may not rule in a consistent manner. Some areas have schedules that are used locally to improve consistency, but in most jurisdictions, the judge who hears your case may be influenced by all sorts of biases regarding the appropriateness of alimony. For instance, we have seen situations in which female judges, who are experienced professionals, do not show a great deal of compassion for women who have chosen to work as full-time moms. There are factors that guide judges' decisions, and we will review those in the chapter that details alimony.

*Child custody* is the unfortunate word used to describe where your children will live and how major decisions about their lives will be made.

We say it is an unfortunate word because "custody" reminds us of property or prisoners, not people we love. It is now becoming common to create a *parenting plan* to detail your custody decisions. This term is much friendlier, in our opinion.

Child custody is often thought of as a win/lose fight, with one parent having the children almost all of the time while the other parent visits periodically. As with alimony, child custody has been revised in the last few decades, but for different reasons. Parents, who in the past may have had limited access to their children, are now typically allowed or asked to play a greater role in their children's lives. This has come about as a result of both lobbying by fathers' rights organizations and evidence that increased involvement by both parents improves outcomes for children of divorce.

Dividing property is a one-time occurrence. When it's done, it's done. Alimony is now usually short term, perhaps lasting a few years. Parenting, though, is an activity and responsibility that may require you and your spouse to work together for more than a decade, depending on the ages of your children. While you will try to foresee what will be best for your children (and you) over time, life will inevitably provide some surprises that will require you to review and revise your parenting plan. You may have to deal with the desire of one spouse to leave the area or a preference expressed by a teenager to live full time with the parent who does not now have primary custody. The main thing you will need to consider as you negotiate and, if necessary, later revise your agreement, is what is in the best interests of your children. Whenever one parent deviates from this guideline, it is likely to create trouble and potentially push the whole process into a courtroom.

The last major issue of divorce you will need to resolve is *child support*. In most cases, the children live with one parent most of the time. Child support is a payment made by the nonresidential parent to the parent with primary custody in order to cover the children's living expenses.

You may actually choose to work on child support first when negotiating your divorce agreement, because it is usually the least contentious of the issues. There are two reasons for this: First, most parents genuinely want to ensure that their children are well cared for. Parents will usually do their best to minimize the impact of their divorce on their children. Second, the federal government has required every state to institute child support guidelines that, in most cases, clearly outline the minimum amount a judge would award for child support. The guidelines vary from state to state, but they do generally make it clear that you can't really avoid being responsible for your kids.

The amount of child support generally depends on the needs of the child, the lifestyle of the family, the number of children, and the income and expenses of the parents. Although the child support guidelines do help reduce the degree of conflict in child support negotiations, keep in mind that they are minimums. You will not want to accept less than the guideline amount. There are many hidden costs in raising children, and if you and your spouse work at identifying these expenses, you may both come to agree that an amount greater than the guideline is fair.

# Finalizing the Divorce

The last major step in the process is finalizing your divorce. In some states, this is a trivial process that can be accomplished by completing forms and mailing or faxing them. In other states, you, or your lawyer, will be required to appear in court. In all cases, if you have negotiated a fair divorce agreement in advance, the process of finalizing the divorce will not be contentious.

Most states require you to wait a certain period of time between separating and finalizing your divorce. Of course, until your divorce is final, you technically remain married and cannot remarry. Although you may feel that, since you have resolved all of the issues, you are safe to act as though you are no longer married, be careful. Laws that apply to married persons still apply to you. In some states, until the divorce is final, your divorce agreement might not be final—so your actions might result in the falling apart of what seemed a done deal.

# Notes

[7] Judith S. Wallerstein and Sandra Blakeslee, *What About the Kids?: Raising Your Children Before, During, and After Divorce* (New York: Hyperion, 2003), 21.

[8] Judith S. Wallerstein and Sandra Blakeslee, *What About the Kids?: Raising Your Children Before, During, and After Divorce* (New York: Hyperion, 2003), 25.

# The Emotions of Divorce

Divorce affects people legally, financially, and emotionally. While we, as lawyers, focus on the legal and financial aspects of divorce, the nature of our specialty requires us to have a strong understanding of what our clients are experiencing emotionally. A lawyer is not a therapist, but good divorce lawyers recognize when strong emotions are at risk of affecting the outcome of a client's divorce. A lawyer can advise you against making poor decisions, but ultimately you must have enough control of your emotions to ensure that your agreement serves both your short-term and long-term interests.

Most people have become comfortable with a "normal" range of emotions, within which they have learned to function well. During divorce, many people find themselves outside of their emotional comfort zone. Even the most even-keeled people may experience a loss of emotional control when faced with the stress of this major transition. In this chapter, we help you understand the emotional aspects of divorce. After describing the emotions you are likely to experience, we offer advice on how you can keep your emotions from interfering with your ability make good long-term decisions while negotiating your divorce agreement. Those who fail to acknowledge and manage their emotions during divorce can easily make a bad situation substantially worse.

## The Range of Emotions

It is important to recognize that divorce is one of the most stressful life events you will experience. Researchers have found that it ranks second only to the death of a spouse.[9] Even going to jail is less stressful than divorce. Approximately 85 percent of divorce decisions are nonmutual--that is, one spouse makes the decision to initiate the divorce. That spouse has had time to begin to adapt to the reality of the impending separation. The initiator is able to control when and how to tell the other spouse about the decision to divorce. Many people are stunned when a spouse announces that the marriage is over, and this shock only makes the potential stress that much worse. Having had time to adjust to the idea of divorce, the initiator is often shocked by the intense reaction of the surprised spouse.

The emotions of divorce are varied, have many causes, and are likely to be confusing, if not completely overwhelming. In the typical case of nonmutual divorce, the initiator is likely to feel frustration, disappointment, and sadness over the perceived failure to achieve the life-long satisfaction once expected from the relationship. If you are the one initiating the divorce, you may also feel guilty that you could not make your marriage work, even though the primary responsibility for the marital problems may not, in fact, belong to you. The feelings of guilt may arise internally or as a result of the comments and actions of your spouse. A spouse who is surprised can react in unexpected ways.

Anger is the emotion most frequently associated with the noninitiating spouse. If you are in this situation and your spouse has had an affair, you are likely to also experience jealousy. Your self-esteem can be seriously wounded, leading to feelings of helplessness and a desire to get back at your spouse. All the while, you too are experiencing the overall sadness of realizing that the dreams and hopes you had for the future must be adjusted. In general, the person who is left behind is more likely to have difficulty with the transition.

Once the initial shock subsides, both spouses usually face stress in adjusting to new routines. A parent who once had support with child care must learn to manage the increased demands of performing household duties without help on most days. This parent may have to do so while transitioning into a new career or school in order to ultimately meet the new financial needs that divorce brings. The spouse who has left the marital residence often deals with loneliness and social isolation. He or she may miss the structure of home life, feeling lost or unconnected to the world.

There are also external sources of stress occurring during separation and divorce. Friends and extended family members may work to influence your decision making. They may attempt to change your mind about your marriage, or they may reinforce any resentment you are feeling toward your spouse. Friends may feel they need to choose sides, perhaps due to pressure from you or your spouse. If that happens and you are not the one who is chosen, you may feel an even greater sense of loss and loneliness. It is also common for joint friends to feel awkward about the situation and become less available at a time when their support might be most valuable.

Anxiety is a normal response to the stress of divorce. One trigger for anxiety in divorce is the fear relating to the ambiguous economic future many people must deal with until their divorce agreement is complete. Indeed, both you and your spouse may have a diminished standard of living for an indefinite period of time, making it necessary to adjust to that new reality. Another significant trigger for anxiety is the fear parents have about how their children will handle the divorce and what arrangements will ultimately be made for their care.

---

# Pseudoreconciliation

It is very common for those thrown into emotional turmoil to return to what has provided them with comfort over the years. We see many cases of what has been referred to as "pseudoreconciliation." This is what happens when the initial positive thoughts a person has about separation—the simplicity of earlier times, adventure, even new romance—turn out to be fleeting. The leaving spouse may instead feel loneliness and guilt. This partner may experience disapproval from friends, parents, and other family members. The result may be a confusing situation wherein the spouse returns home and even goes on to feel much better for a while. Usually though, unless substantial work is done to improve the relationship, the problems that led to separation recur, and the couple separates again.

This pattern, which sometimes repeats, is traumatic for the adults and can be much more traumatic for any involved children, who have likely fantasized about their parents reconciling.

## The Grieving Process

Divorce is comparable to the experience of grieving over the death of a loved one. We all understand such grief as a painful process that we go through but from which we eventually recover. The stages, identified by Elisabeth Kubler-Rosss in her book *On Death and Dying*, are:

- Shock and denial
- Anger
- Depression
- Bargaining
- Sorrow
- Understanding and acceptance

While the experience of the leaver can be quite different than that of the person who is left, you are likely to feel yourself going through most of those stages regardless of your role. The divorce recovery or adjustment process typically takes from one to four years. Some people, usually men, can rearrange their lives a bit faster. Others have great difficulty and need even more time to let go, establish a new identity, rebuild their social ties, and adapt to a new parenting role. The important thing to know is that, although divorce can be extremely painful, people do get through it.

## Emotional Readiness for Negotiation

We hope you now recognize the many emotions that are likely to arise as a result of your divorce. Our concern is that you recognize and respect what is happening as you go through this transition. Most everyone can remember things they did when they were infatuated or first in love that now seem silly or nonproductive. In hindsight, it is easy to see how our emotions, rather than our rational thinking, were in control. That's life. If we were completely rational all the time, life would be rather dull.

During divorce, you must take stock of and work to manage your emotions in a way you may never have had to before. If you focus too much on immediate gratification of emotional urges, you may be disserving your long-term goals of emotional stability and financial security. For instance, if you were not the initiator of the divorce, you may be terribly angry and have a powerful urge to punish your spouse for what he or she has done to you. Acting on your anger at your spouse will almost surely reduce the chances for an amicable, cooperative settlement. Worse, a flaring of tensions could precipitate an ugly and unnecessary court battle. Growth can be very hard work; we know this. But you can't learn from this process if you aren't willing to do that work.

While in most cases the noninitiator goes into the divorce process feeling angry, the initiator may experience a great deal of guilt. We have seen initiators whose guilt or desire to get things over quickly (possibly in an effort to skip the grieving process) prompted them to make unwise concessions. Some have been willing to provide lifetime alimony, causing themselves a lifelong, and potentially unnecessary, major financial burden.

The transition of divorce can be broken down into many stages, but there are two milestones that are most critical when it comes to working constructively toward an amicable settlement, which, as we will discuss in detail later, is the option that will best serve nearly everyone going through divorce. The first milestone is reached when you have developed enough emotional distance from your spouse to be able to rationally consider your needs and the realistic possibilities available to you with regard to finances and the care of your children. If your thinking about what you want in your divorce agreement is primarily driven by the pain it will cause your spouse or the guilt you are feeling for ending the marriage, negotiations are likely to fail or result in an agreement you will later regret.

The second milestone is a shift in mindset regarding the relationship. While many people adopt a hostile stance at the beginning of divorce, others, particularly those who are surprised by the divorce, have trouble separating themselves enough from the relationship to think of their own best interests. Most people for whom divorce comes as a surprise are at a disadvantage because the initiating spouse has already changed from an "us" to a "me" mindset. Initiating spouses are thinking about their own best interests. The person who is caught off guard has spent years thinking of the couple as "us." It can be difficult to quickly change gears from an "us" to a "me" kind of mentality in order to make better decisions.

If your spouse initiated the divorce, it may take you some time to believe that it is really happening. You might think your spouse is acting impulsively and will reverse course. Because divorce came suddenly to you, it may seem that it was an impulsive decision by your spouse. In most cases though, the spouse who initiates divorce has planned it for months before revealing the decision. Even while you're working with a lawyer to draft a divorce agreement, you may still believe that your spouse is just going through a midlife crisis, which will end, soon, with reconciliation. You may think that your decisions don't really matter because they're not permanent. It is important to consider how far ahead your spouse may be in making these decisions. He or she is most likely making sound long-term decisions for his or her benefit. You need to do the same.

Just as with negotiating while ruled by anger, negotiating without developing an independent view of yourself and your needs can be dangerous. Rather than thinking of their own needs, people in this situation are prone to make decisions intended to placate their spouses, expecting them to "snap out of it" and come back. If you feel willing to offer anything in order to save the marriage and return whatever comfort you previously had, you may be in the bargaining stage of the grieving process. Both parties need to be careful about promises or arrangements made under these circumstances, as they may be unrealistic and eventually result in more suffering for one or both of you.

If you have significant assets, substantially different incomes, or children, the financial decisions you and your spouse make during divorce may be the most important of your lives. They can have major short-term and long-term impacts. It is important that anyone making these decisions be as prepared as possible. To improve the chances of settlement, each spouse needs to get far enough through the initial emotional up-heaval of divorce, before beginning negotiations, to work constructively with the other party. At the same time, you need to have made enough of an identity adjustment—from being part of a married couple to being an independent person—that you can clearly identify your own needs.

It is in the best interests of each spouse to give the other the time nec-essary to reach the emotional milestones we have highlighted here before negotiations begin. It may be impractical to wait until understanding and acceptance occur, but divorcing partners need to be past anger, not be mired in depression, and able to consider their own best interests. Some-times, though, one spouse, or the respective lawyer, fails to understand the importance of waiting for the timing to be right before moving for-ward with the legal and financial aspects of divorce. When this happens, it may be necessary for a lawyer representing the spouse who needs more time to step in and use legal procedures to slow things down. In cases in which we see spouses having trouble making these shifts, we try to slow things down and often recommend that our client use the time to get therapy to accelerate their emotional preparation for negotiations.

---

## Reaching Emotional Readiness

Many people start off on the wrong foot emotionally in divorce. They try to deny their grief and act as if everything is fine. They may dive into many new activities, start another relationship right away, or use drugs or alcohol to avoid dealing with their pain. These coping strategies can lead to trouble. You need to allow yourself to experience your grief fully in order to progress through it. Crying is a natural way to deal with the intense emotions you're likely feeling. If you have children, get some help to care for them so you can have time alone to express your sadness with-out feeling that you need to be stoic.

Regardless of how gracefully you do or don't accept the initial realiza-tion that your marriage is over, you will still have to work through all the stages of coping with your new reality. The question is how you are going to get to each of those emotional milestones. For some people, time will be an adequate healer. These folks can progress through the stages of divorce at a pace that allows them to deal with the legal and financial aspects as and when necessary. For others, any numbers of motivations (anger, a spouse's desire to move forward quickly, a need for certainty, the desire to remarry) may make it necessary to accelerate the process of getting emotionally ready for negotiations.

As you go through divorce, you will need the help of others. You may feel that you can go it alone, and you might very well be able to—but ask yourself why you would want to. Divorce isn't a contest. Your goal should be to make an emotional transition that causes as little pain for yourself and others as possible. Reaching out for help, or simply accepting it when it is offered, will yield the best results. One of the life lessons that sometimes comes from a divorce is the recognition that we all need a community of friends to rely on in tough times.

We mentioned earlier that friends may feel awkward once they know about the divorce. Some will feel they need to choose sides, perhaps because of who they knew first. Others will not be sure what to say when you see them. You may need to reach out and begin the discourse. Ideally, you want to identify the family members and friends you can rely on as part of your emotional support system. Those who will help you most are those who listen well. Someone who reinforces your anger or plays devil's advocate will drain your energy rather than helping you heal and move on.

If you don't feel you have a supportive listener among your friends and family, you may need to find a support group that can help. These days, there are support groups for people experiencing every kind of difficulty in life, including divorce. In our state, most of these groups meet in churches but are nondenominational. You can probably find groups where you are with a quick Internet search.

People going through a divorce can easily get stuck in an emotional rut. The usual routine can be tiring, depressing, or just uninspiring. If you feel that you aren't making progress toward reaching the emotional milestones we discussed, try to break out of your normal routine. You may need to stop thinking about your divorce for a while in order to gain some perspective and find some peace. Set your sights on the future by getting involved in an activity that will inspire you and help you see that there is more to life than what you are experiencing right now. Here are some ideas:

- Take a class in a field you have always been interested in.
- Try a new hobby.
- Read an uplifting book.
- Take a short vacation.
- Volunteer for a cause or organization that will make you feel great for helping.
- Explore your spiritual side.
- Go for a walk in nature.

We are also huge fans of regular exercise. The mind-body connection is well documented. Feeling good physically leads to feeling good mentally. During long runs, bike rides, and swims, your mind has time to process all that is happening in your life and help you put it in perspective. The best way we've found to get people exercising is to get them to sign up for some type of race. You don't have to win a race to benefit. Just having a goal, training for it, and accomplishing it can greatly improve your sense of well-being and improve your self-esteem. You are also likely to get outside and meet people who are in good spirits.

From lifestyle columnists, you may read the advice to jump back in the relationship game soon after breaking up. We, and most other experts, recommend avoiding new relationships for a year or more. If you are already seeing someone or do get involved with a new person, do your best to keep the relationship from becoming too serious. Many people, especially men, marry within a year or two of divorce. These marriages have a very high divorce rate, primarily because not enough effort was put into learning from the mistakes of the first marriage. It's best to avoid compounding your pain.

---

## Dealing with Depression and Anxiety

Everyone going through divorce experiences many of the emotions we described earlier. For some, depression or anxiety continues long enough to keep them from effectively managing the legal and financial decisions that must be made during divorce. Without the help of a mental health professional, people dealing with depression and anxiety suffer needlessly. They may additionally make decisions they later regret and increase the cost of their divorce by attempting to use their lawyer as a therapist.

Depression is so common for people going through divorce that we feel everyone should do a regular self-assessment to help differentiate between the depression that is part of all grieving and more serious clinical depression, which is best alleviated by treatment from a mental health professional. The most common quick screening for depression is to consider how many of the following symptoms you are experiencing:

- Persistent sad, anxious, or "empty" mood
- Sleeping too much or too little with middle-of-the-night or early-morning waking
- Reduced appetite and weight loss, or increased appetite and weight gain
- Loss of pleasure and interest in activities once enjoyed, including sex (although that may be hard to judge, since you may not be having much sex at this point)
- Restlessness, irritability
- Persistent physical symptoms that do not respond to treatment (such as chronic pain or digestive disorders)
- Difficulty concentrating, remembering, or making decisions
- Fatigue or loss of energy
- Feeling guilty, hopeless, or worthless
- Thoughts of suicide or death

The presence of five or more of these symptoms for two weeks or more is an indicator that you may have a type of depression that could benefit from treatment with therapy and, possibly, medication.

Anxiety is another condition you need to look out for during this stressful time. Everybody experiences the symptoms of anxiety from time to time. Most people dealing with depression will experience anxiety. Others may experience anxiety without being depressed.

Anxiety becomes a problem when it is experienced intensely and when it persistently interferes with a person's daily life. Frequent feelings of inner tension, agitation, fear of losing control, dread of a catastrophic event, irritability, or being detached from the world are some of the psychological symptoms of anxiety. The condition has many physical symptoms as well, including a racing heart, shortness of breath, chest tightness, dry mouth, butterflies in the stomach, tremor, and sweating.

The treatment for both depression and anxiety can involve psychotherapy or medication or both. Psychotherapy, sometimes referred to as talk therapy, is a technique for helping people identify the factors contributing to their depression and effectively deal with the psychological, behavioral, interpersonal, and situational causes. Therapy can help ease the pain of depression and the feelings of hopelessness it brings. It should also reduce the pessimism, unrealistic expectations, and overly critical self-evaluations that create and sustain depression.

In all but the most severe cases, the use of medication is optional. When medication is used, it is usually in combination with psychotherapy, because the medication does not solve the problems that lead to the depression or anxiety. Combining medication with psychotherapy can be useful because some symptoms of depression—such as sleep and appetite disturbances, significant concentration problems, and chronic fatigue— interfere with your ability to make the life changes necessary to eliminate the depression. Antidepressant medication can help relieve those symptoms and allow you to make needed life changes.

If you are experiencing depression while going through divorce, it is important that you get help. We also urge you to at least consider using medication to speed your treatment. You might prefer to resolve any mental health issues you have strictly by talking with a counselor. You might have an aversion to the idea of "quick fix" solutions. But using psychotherapy alone may not be the fastest, most effective for you to work your way out of this particular slough of despond. Divorce is a major crisis, and you may need to handle things differently than you ever would have before.

Using medication during this time does not mean you will need to use it forever. It's not a lifetime decision. However, the legal and financial decisions you make during your divorce may indeed be with you forever. If you are the more dependent spouse, you may never again be in a position to obtain any significant amount of money from your ex. If you have children, significant assets, and potential for receiving or paying alimony—and you are unable to unable to use good judgment because of the anxiety or stress—you will want to use whatever resources are available to help you make good decisions. Once you get past the critical legal and financial aspects in the divorce, you can work on the underlying causes of your mental health issues. You might also find that issues go away when the divorce decisions are resolved.

## Obstacles to Getting Help

Concerns about confidentiality sometimes keep people from getting mental health help. These concerns can be legitimate but are usually outweighed by the benefits of the care received. Many people are worried about whether an employer can learn of any illness if they use benefits provided by their company to pay for their visits. This will vary depending on how your company handles its benefits. You have the choice of discussing the issue with your benefits administrator or, if you are uncomfortable even doing that, paying out of pocket for your mental health care.

Many recent legal changes have been designed to improve the privacy of medical information. However, not every office or company follows the new rules consistently, so you need to be cautious about the individuals and organizations who have access to your information. Ask how confidential information is protected and don't sign blanket medical record release forms. Only sign time-limited requests to release specific information. For therapy to be as effective as possible, you must be able to trust that sensitive information discussed with your therapist will not be shared with others.

Another concern regarding mental health confidentiality arises when a couple with children is unable to agree on how to handle child custody. In most states, information revealed in counseling can be used by your spouse to show that you might not provide the best care for the children. Judges have generally ruled that determining what is best for the children is more important than the patient's right to confidentiality. It is usually best for people to get the mental health care they need, because without care, the symptoms they are experiencing could cause poor decision making as well as all sorts of other problems. However, if you are in this type of situation, you need to talk to a lawyer to understand how the law works in your state and consider the pros and cons of getting help. One thing to remember is that mental illnesses, such as depression, are very common and, when treated, may not have a major impact on a judge's determination of your fitness to parent.

Those who lack insurance or who choose not to use it because of their concerns about confidentiality sometimes fail to get the professional help they need, feeling that they cannot afford it. What they often don't realize is that they will spend much more on legal fees—making bad judgments and spending time relying on their lawyer for emotional support—than they would have on some therapy, and perhaps medication. It is very short sighted not to use any appropriate solution you can.

Finally, some people, particularly the initiators of the divorce, avoid getting help because they simply don't perceive that they have a problem. The initiator may not experience the depression common to the noninitiator, but this person still had a marriage that didn't work out. Usually this spouse believes that the failure of the marriage was entirely the fault of the other spouse. Unfortunately, many people go through multiple failed relationships before realizing they need to get some help. Rather than waiting, they would better off exploring the underlying issues as they engage in the divorce process so as to deal with these issues effectively and have a better chance in future relationships. As we said before, the only way to find the silver lining of divorce is to do the difficult emotional work required for growth and change.

---

# Finding a Mental Health Professional

If you have made the decision to get help from a mental health professional, the first issue you face is determining which type of professional to choose. The types of mental health professionals you may encounter when looking for help include:

- Psychiatrists: Psychiatrists are medical doctors who specialize in the study, treatment, and prevention of mental disorders. After earning their medical degree, they complete a four-year residency. Because they're medical doctors, psychiatrists can prescribe medications as part of mental health treatment. Psychiatrists vary in the amount of counseling (talk therapy) they perform.

- Psychologists: Psychologists usually have a doctorate degree. They undergo at least four years of training and education in research, human behavioral theories, and therapeutic techniques. They may also have a year or more of post-doctoral supervised training or practice. Psychologists provide therapy and counseling, administer psychological assessments, and perform research. Clinical psychologists work with the diagnosis and treatment of mental disorders. Counseling psychologists focus mainly on adjustment issues or life challenges, such as divorce.

- Clinical Social Workers: Clinical social workers are the largest group of professionally trained mental health care providers in the United States. Licensed clinical social workers (LCSW) have a master's degree in social work (MSW) along with additional clinical training. An LCSW can provide a full range of mental health services, including assessment, diagnosis, and treatment. They draw on a variety of psychotherapeutic theories and tools to help individuals, couples, families, and groups deal with emotional problems, mental disorders, and substance abuse/chemical dependency.

- Counselors: Like social workers, counselors have a master's degree, usually in counseling. State requirements to become a licensed professional counselor (LPC) are varied but typically require one to three years of supervised experience and passage of an examination.

- Pastoral Counselors: A pastoral counselor is a member of the clergy who integrates religious concepts with training in behavioral science. Licensing is not required, but counselors can seek certification with the American Association of Pastoral Counselors.

We listed psychiatrists and psychologists first because they have the most advanced training. If your symptoms are severe, someone in one of those fields is likely to be your best first choice. If your condition could benefit from medication, you may want to consider a psychiatrist who specializes in both medical treatment and psychotherapy. You may choose to work with two professionals: one who focuses on psychotherapy and a psychiatrist or your medical doctor for any medication that may be required.

The provisions of your insurance coverage may dictate the type of therapist you choose. If you are using insurance to pay for your treatment, you will need to contact the carrier and determine what types of therapists are covered and how many visits are allowed. Fees for psychiatrists are generally the highest, so visits to them may be limited.

Finding a therapist who is right for you can be difficult, especially since you aren't at your best—or you wouldn't be looking for help. Each of the professions listed above have websites where you can find listings of therapists in your area. Consider getting help from your doctor, family, or friends. Because the therapist relationship is such a personal one, you really need to find someone you are comfortable with. This will probably require talking to two, three, or more therapists over the phone and then choosing one or two to visit in person. If insurance coverage is a major factor, you will want to consider if the referrals accept the type of insurance you have.

Be aware that while you may have chosen someone you felt you could relate well to, the first few visits may be upsetting or disappointing. This is not unusual. More than one session may be needed to build a sense of trust between you and the therapist. If you still feel uncomfortable after a number of sessions, talk to the therapist about your concerns and be willing to make a change if those concerns are not resolved.

# Notes

[9] Thomas H. Holmes and Richard H. Rahe, "The Social Readjustment Rating Scale," *Journal of Psychosomatic Research* 11 no. 2 (1967): 213-18.

# Divorce and Finances

Many people are very uncomfortable making financial decisions. Others enjoy actively managing their money, especially when they have time to research and make a single decision at a time. During a divorce, though, you may need to make a number of financial decisions within a relatively short period of time. Of the four major issues of divorce—property division, alimony, child custody, and child support—three are primarily focused on money. You cannot afford to go through a divorce without gaining a solid understanding of your financial picture and being able to assess how the things in your divorce agreement will affect you financially.

The first financial decisions you will make as part of your divorce revolve around what to do within the first few weeks after you and your spouse discuss the decision to separate. This is a period during which there usually is no formal agreement specifying how you will manage your money. There are a number of risks that need to be considered, along with actions that you may need to take to reduce or eliminate these risks. For instance, will your spouse go on a spending spree on a joint credit card? Alternatively, would closing joint accounts ratchet up the level of animosity between you, thus reducing the chances of an amicable settlement?

After the initial period of separation, you will begin negotiating your divorce agreement. This chapter helps you build the foundation you will need to have in place prior to making those decisions.

# Collecting Your Financial Information

In a very real sense, knowledge and information are power. If your spouse has information that you never discover, he or she can, and all too often will, walk away with more property than the law would award. If the noncustodial spouse does not disclose accurate income information, the custodial spouse may wind up receiving monthly child support that is below the amount specified in the state's child support guidelines. Similarly, if you have been financially dependent, and you underestimate your spouse's actual income, your expectations for short- or long-term financial assistance might be lower than they should be.

The first thing you can do—and the first thing you must do as soon as you know that your marriage is ending—is to collect all the financial records and other asset or debt information that you know exist. If you are the designated financial manager in the household, you may already know where all such information is. If you have had little to do with the family finances, use the sections later in this chapter to help you figure these things out.

If some financial documents are papers in file folders at your home, make copies and then store the copies in a safe place outside the house, such as a lawyer's office, an individual safe-deposit box, or the home of a trusted friend or relative. If other records are on your home computer, make copies of all of them. If you don't know how to use the computer, prevail on a friend to help you. It is not unusual for one spouse to come home one day and discover that the other spouse has removed all written records or computer files and taken them to an undisclosed location. Don't get caught in such a situation!

Some spouses do not begin to gather and copy the family's financial records out of fear that the other spouse will catch on to what is happening, causing an already bad situation to get much worse. While this fear is understandable, records to which you have access can usually be copied discreetly, thus minimizing the risk of an explosion with your spouse. More importantly, the risk of new conflict is not usually a good enough reason not to act to safeguard personal financial information.

In the situation of separation and divorce, it is more often a far greater risk to you to not have financial information than to irritate your spouse if he or she happens to learn that you have made copies of relevant family documents. One critical exception to this occurs in the family with domestic violence. If just about anything will make your spouse physically violent and put either you or your children in danger, you need to leave and worry about the documents later.

Many spouses who have had little to do with handling money in the family need considerable encouragement to get energized to collect documents and records. The barrier to obtaining family financial records is sometimes as much psychological as it is logistical, since a spouse who has been kept in the dark about finances sometimes has low self-esteem and paralyzing feelings of powerlessness. If you are feeling fearful or powerless, you need to deal with those feelings immediately so that you can take the action you might be keeping yourself from taking. Strong feelings are feelings that other people can help you deal with and surmount.

Financial and other property records that you know about and can copy might disappear before you take action. All these records are too valuable to ignore. If you don't make the copies now, you will either spend tons of money later on—employing an attorney to force the documents to be disclosed, all the while knowing that everything may not be disclosed in the end—or find yourself forced to settle on terms potentially more unfavorable than you will ever know. Taking prompt actions now will spare untold later expense and headache in securing access to necessary financial information. Don't worry about making sense of the documents you collect. Understanding financial documents may require the assistance of a professional with financial skills and sophistication. Such assistance is available; first, you have to have the documents.

Clients who have little knowledge of financial affairs often ask us how to go about gathering such documents. One way is to think whether there is any stretch of time when your spouse will be predictably at work or, even better, out of town, allowing you a longer period to, with reduced anxiety, sort through papers in your house. As you do your hunting, you might want to be careful to put the papers back in the same order and in the same place you found them, thus lessening the chance that a controlling spouse will spot your temporary "borrowing" for purposes of having the documents copied.

If you have not been involved in managing your finances, the amount of information you need to collect to ensure you have a complete picture can be overwhelming. You will want to use file folders, binders, or some other method to organize what you collect. This will help anyone who works with you on your finances to get up to speed quickly, thereby saving you money.

We also remind clients, over and over, that all the background work they do for themselves is that much more money saved in lawyer's fees, given that most attorneys charge by the hour. So, even if you intend to use an attorney for your separation and divorce, the more information gathering you do on your own, the more you will have streamlined the work a lawyer needs to conduct on your case. You will also be a more knowledgeable, and hence more powerful, ally to yourself—and your attorney—in negotiating a favorable settlement when you have become acquainted with the financial records.

## Assembling Your Complete Financial Picture

There are few times in our lives when we have to document all of our assets and liabilities, in addition to our income. While many people are aware of their income and expenses, few that come to us for help with divorce regularly track their net worth. You will need to understand your income, your expenses, *and* your net worth as you proceed in your divorce negotiations. In the next sections, we help you identify all of the pieces of your financial puzzle so you can create the complete picture you need.

### Income

Documenting current income for most people is straightforward. If you or your spouse is employed, you will want a recent paystub from each job. This normally includes information about the current pay period as well as year-to-date information. If you or your spouse owns a business, you will need to determine the income generated from the business as well as its value as an asset for the sake of considering property division. We discuss this further in the business information section below.

People's income fluctuates from year to year as a result of job changes, promotions, commissions, bonuses, or other factors. Because the income you or your spouse currently receives may not be representative of what you have received recently or can expect to receive in the future, you will want to collect state and federal income tax returns for at least the last five years, so that you can document income trends. Another useful item if you wind up in court can be copies of your spouse's resume. In some cases, a spouse expecting to pay alimony may temporarily take a job with lower pay in an effort to reduce alimony payments. A resume may be useful in documenting such a ploy.

Income tax returns are useful for more than documenting changes in compensation; they also identify other sources of income that may not be evident. For instance, an investment account that your spouse may not have mentioned recently may generate income that is listed on the return.

If your taxes have not been filed for the current year, you will want a copy of all W-2s that will be used for filing. If any cannot be located, attempt to get a copy of the final paystub from the previous year, which would include year-to-date compensation information. While we will discuss more about businesses later, if you or your spouse works as a contractor, there may be several 1099 (miscellaneous income) forms showing income produced in the prior year.

## Real Estate

For most married couples, their home is their largest asset. If you own a home, you will need to know its purchase price, its current value, how much equity you have in it (the value minus any loans), and what it costs to own the property. Although an appraisal is the most reliable way to determine current market value of property, you can ask a real estate agent to give you a market evaluation. Most agents are happy to provide this service, in the hope they will be selected to sell your house. If you and your spouse use professionals to determine the value independently, it is unlikely that your valuations will differ greatly.

You will need to document any mortgages, home equity loans, and home equity lines of credit secured by the house. For each loan, you will need the lender's name, the original amount, the current principal balance, and your monthly payment. This information can be obtained on a recent statement for each loan or by contacting the lender. Many lenders provide this information via their websites. If this is not the case with yours, you can call to get it.

Owning property comes with an obligation to pay property tax. If you have a mortgage, you are also probably required to have homeowner's insurance. Payments for taxes and insurance are often paid with your mortgage payment into an escrow account managed by your lender. If that's not the case, you will need to know how much the taxes and insurance are so that you can add them to your budget.

You will need this same information for each property you own. To avoid confusion, separate the information for each property into its own folder, labeled with its address.

## Vehicles

Vehicles, including automobiles, recreational vehicles, motorcycles, boats, and trailers can also have significant value. Start by getting a copy of the title for each vehicle. You will also need to know the value of these vehicles. One source of automobile values is the Kelley Blue Book.

Among many services, the site offers vehicle valuations for free. You can also find this book and similar publications at car dealerships and public libraries.

Most vehicle values decrease over time. Classic cars may need to be appraised, although some specialized publications cover this area of collecting. You will want to determine the value of the vehicles at the time of separation. Waiting many months or more could lead to a dispute about what value should be used. If you use a book to determine values, make sure you are using an edition valid for the time you separated. Make sure you photocopy the information you use to justify your valuation.

In distributing your property, the amount of property you brought into the marriage may be significant. Because of this, you will want to document any loan balance as of your marriage date as well as the balance as of the date of separation. If the vehicle was owned outright at the time of marriage, note that.

If a lawyer will help you with your negotiations, you will want to indicate who uses each vehicle, as most couples wish to keep their respective vehicles after the divorce.

## Household Items

People often have misconceptions about the value of their household items and appliances. We find that our clients are sometimes surprised at how little individual items are worth (from a fair-market-value point of view, i.e., what they would sell for in a garage sale or on eBay) versus what they cost new. On the other hand, houses are filled with so many items that their cumulative value becomes significant. Further, if one spouse is required to furnish a new household, he or she will usually buy new items, therefore paying what is called replacement costs. In dividing property, a court would consider fair-market value, but if you are negotiating an agreement, you will want to keep in mind what it will cost to replace a refrigerator, dining room set, or other items that may get traded away.

Make an inventory of your household items and appliances. You may want to focus only on items worth a few hundred dollars or more, but you can get as detailed as you like. Make note of items that are of special value to you, either for sentimental reasons or for financial reasons, so that you or your attorney can try to keep or get them. If any of your household items were purchased on payment plans, you will need to determine the balance due and indicate those balances on your list.

## Collectibles and Antiques

Items such as stamp and coin collections, jewelry, antique furniture, oriental rugs, fine art, and the like need to be listed and valued. Many collectibles have more value to their owner than to others; but in a divorce, the owner has an incentive to indicate they have less value than they do. You will want to know the real fair-market value of each item but also to consider how dear an item may be to your spouse as you negotiate. If you are using a lawyer to help in negotiations, you will need to alert him or her to things you or your spouse consider especially valuable. To determine the fair-market value of items you may try eBay, looking at completed sales of similar items. For particularly valuable items, you will need to find a professional appraiser specializing in the type of item to be valued.

## Bank Accounts and Credit Cards

If you or your spouse uses a computer program to manage your personal finances, do whatever is possible to get a copy of the data files. The files will, at a minimum, have information on your bank accounts. Many people track credit and investment accounts in these programs as well, so you could save yourself a lot of work with these files.

You need to document your bank accounts. You will want to know the financial institution, the type of account, and the balance on the date of separation. Bank statements and cancelled checks for the last twelve months will be helpful to fully document the activity of your account. Reviewing your spending will be critical when you need to develop your budget for life after divorce. As with the bank accounts, you will want the balance at the date of separation and the last year of statements for any credit cards you and your spouse use.

Certificates of deposit are another asset you may have purchased through your bank. These certificates have a denomination, interest rate, and maturity date that you will need to determine.

## Student Loans

Student loans are, obviously, just another variety of debt that you need to consider as you build your list of assets and debts. You will want the name of the lender, the amount due, and the required monthly payment. Remember that loans taken out by either spouse are significant to your overall financial picture.

## Tax Refunds and Debts

While many of us dread April 15, some people find that tax time offers a nice surprise in the form of a refund. If you are compiling your assets at a time when you or your spouse may be due a refund from the IRS, you need to consider this money as an asset. If your tax return has not yet been filed for the year, the information you are collecting for your divorce negotiations should help in completing the return or having a certified public accountant (CPA) do it for you.

Those working without regular paychecks usually have to file estimated taxes on a quarterly basis. It is not uncommon for people to either fail to make these payments or underpay the amount. This is one way people end up with a tax bill they cannot pay on time. The IRS works out payment plans with a large number of payers. If you or your spouse has a debt to the IRS, you need to determine the amount of the debt as well as any arrangements that have been agreed to regarding periodic payments.

## Safe-Deposit Boxes

If you and your spouse have one or more safe-deposit boxes, you should, at a minimum, inventory their contents. The box(es) may contain important financial documents along with valuable collectibles or jewelry. Depending on your situation, you may want to remove the items or get both keys to the box to avoid your spouse removing the contents. If this is not feasible, you can protect yourself by photographing the items and having a bank officer sign your inventory. In an extreme case, your lawyer could get a restraining order from a judge and provide a copy to the bank to prevent you or your spouse opening the box until the order is removed.

## Leases, Contracts, and Other Obligations

If you are not a home owner, you and your spouse are likely to have a lease, committing you to pay rent for some time into the future. You will need to locate this document to know the duration of your commitment. Other obligations you will want to consider could include the rent on a storage unit, a contract on a security system, or installment contracts for purchases of household furnishings or appliances.

## Investment Accounts

If either you or your spouse has investment accounts, you will want to collect statements showing the name of the financial institution, the name on the accounts, the type of account, and the holdings in the account along with valuation on the date of separation.

## Life Insurance

Life insurance is another asset that needs to be considered in divorce. You will need to know the insurance company, the name of the insured, the face amount, the beneficiary, the type of policy (term, whole life, universal), the cash surrender value—if any—as of the date of separation, and the amount of any outstanding loan amounts. Again, you should be able to find all of this information on the most recent statement from the company.

## Retirement Plans

Retirement plans can be one of the most complex assets in a divorce because, depending on the type of plan or plans, it may be difficult to determine their current value. While most of the time we advise our clients to trade items or cash of equal value instead of dividing retirement plans, sometimes the plan is a large asset that must be divided in order to create a settlement. This process can be complicated by the fact that many types of plans require a special court order for division called a Qualified Domestic Relations Order (QDRO). We will talk more about this in the chapter on property distribution.

When you are working to find out about the existence and value of your retirement plans, remember that you or your spouse may have retirement benefits, which could be significant, owed to you through prior jobs. An older person who has been married for many years needs to consider the entire work history of his or her spouse to make sure no benefits that might have been accrued in an earlier job are missing. Document all pension, retirement (401k, IRA), and profit-sharing plans and accounts. You will want to know the name of the plan or account, how long it was held, the number of years required for vesting, the earliest possible retirement date, the participant's birth date, hire date, and the termination date if applicable. This is the type of information that an attorney, actuary, CPA, or other professional can use to help you determine the value of such plans.

## Stock Options

Stock options became very popular during the late 1990s boom, particularly among those in the technology industry. Surprisingly, many people did not, and may still not, have a good understanding of their stock options. We had one client come to us who had been so focused on working that he had never taken the time to calculate the value of his options. He was amazed when we told him that they were worth millions. Imagine being the spouse of someone in this situation and not doing the extra legwork required to find out about the stock options. You could unknowingly leave millions of dollars out of your settlement.

The way options are handled varies from company to company. Also, courts vary in how they value options, whether they consider options to be an asset subject to division, and how the options affect any support a spouse might be required to pay. You will most likely need to get advice on your specific situation from a lawyer. To help a lawyer or other professional determine the value of the stock options, you will need to provide the original stock option plan and all amendments. People receive grant agreements whenever given stock options. You will need all of those agreements. There should be a stock options summary statement, showing information about each grant, including whether grants have been exercised or sold or both. Stocks in growing companies sometimes split, which means that the number of shares granted may have increased at some point. This may explain any difference between the shares listed on the grant agreements and in the summary statement.

## Marriage and Divorce Agreements

If you and your spouse made an agreement regarding your partnership before (prenuptial) or during (postnuptial) your marriage, you will obviously need those documents in order to understand your options during divorce negotiations. Similarly, since a prior divorce agreement or judgment could affect you or your spouse's finances due to ongoing support payments, you will need a copy of such a document. If your spouse has the burden of paying support, you will want to identify the duration of the arrangement, including any triggers (such as the former spouse's remarriage) that might affect the agreement.

## Estate-Planning Documents

Although they may not affect you during your divorce negotiations, you will want to locate copies of any estate-planning documents, including wills and trusts. These documents will require modification after your divorce, and you may even wish to modify them during your separation.

## Business Information

Valuing businesses is difficult. In most cases, an accountant or business appraiser will be needed to help. The information you will need to determine the value of the business includes the most recent financial statement, the most recent profit-and-loss statement, the annual profit-and-loss statements, tax returns, shares owned (if a corporation), names of officers and shareholders (if applicable), net worth, and formation documents, such as partnership agreements or corporate by-laws and charters. These documents reflect what has been reported by the company.

Unfortunately, it's not just large businesses that "cook the books." In an effort to minimize taxes or, if they know a divorce-related valuation is coming, hide or delay income in various ways, some business owners may resort to one or more of the following tactics:

- Delaying depositing checks.
- Increasing expenses by adding nonworking employees to payroll.
- Increasing expenses by paying for personal items or automobiles with business funds.
- Delaying billing clients for projects.
- Delaying signing long-term contracts.

If you suspect any of these activities, then you may need a forensic accountant to go through the details of the business to determine what is really going on. However, because these specialized accounts are expensive, the costs of their services could be greater than what you might gain. You will need to use your judgment, potentially in consultation with an attorney, to determine whether such an investigation is worth the cost.

---

# Finding Missing Financial Information

If your spouse is uncooperative and you are unable to locate your records, one thing you can do to identify the companies involved in your financial life is to watch the mail. You may be able to learn the names of your bank, insurance companies, credit card and mortgage lenders, and investment companies. Once you know the companies involved, you should be able to call them to order copies of your account information.

Some financial documents contain a bounty of financial information, so you may want to make them a priority if you are having trouble tracking things down. In particular, look for loan applications, particularly an application used for a mortgage or refinancing. Those applications will include information about other assets and debts of which you may not be aware. Similarly, loans taken out for business purposes will likely yield a wealth of information. A home loan application may be stored with your home closing documents. Many of these documents are on longer, legal-size paper, so they may be kept outside of a standard file drawer.

Checking registers for a personal account or a business account represents another potential gateway to further information. These registers can provide you with critical details you will need for working out a budget for life after divorce. You are also likely to be able to find a record of outstanding loans that your spouse may be paying down, investment/retirement accounts that he or she may be putting money into, and insurance companies that may have policies of value to you.

Finally, credit reports provide information about current and past financial connections you and your spouse may jointly have. Credit reports cover an individual, but if you have a joint credit account, information about the account is reported on both individuals' credit reports. So, while you may not be able to get the full financial record of a spouse you may find information you were not previously aware of in your credit report.

There are three main credit reporting agencies: Equifax, Experian, and Transunion. In several states, it is possible to get a copy of your credit report for free—this will soon apply nationwide. However, you may find different information on the reports from each agency. Rather than dealing with each agency independently, you may find it worthwhile to buy a credit report from one agency that includes the reports from the other two. All three agencies currently provide this service. You can also enroll in a service that updates you if information in your report changes. This is typically sold as a way to help you know if your identity has been stolen. However, as your information may be changing throughout the divorce process, it can be useful to tune in to your credit reports more carefully than you might have otherwise, in this way ensuring nothing negative occurs as a result of changes to your joint accounts.

## Documenting Separate Property

Although there are two major approaches to dividing property, all fifty states recognize the concept of separate property. In general, this is property that was owned by one spouse prior to the marriage, received as a gift specifically for one spouse, acquired through inheritance, or acquired after the date of separation. Separate property that is mixed with marital property (perhaps by making loan payments with marital funds) may become completely or partially marital property. You will want to do your best to document any assets you may have had prior to the marriage so that you, most likely with the assistance of a lawyer, can determine if they can be categorized as separate. On the other hand, if you expect your spouse to claim property, potentially including a business, as separate property, you will want to gather documentation to show any contributions made to the property during the marriage.

## Protecting Your Finances

Whether you are just learning the details of your finances or have always been the money manager in your relationship, you need to be aware that the period from the time the divorce process begins until the divorce is finalized is a particularly risky time when it comes to finances. You will need to determine what needs to be done to protect each of your assets while you negotiate your divorce agreement and await your final divorce. You will also want to protect or enhance your credit rating so that you will be able to borrow money in the future for a new house, a car, or other expenses.

One of the first things you will want to consider is closing joint credit accounts, including credit cards, home equity lines of credit, and brokerage margin accounts. If you cannot pay off the balances, you will not be able to close the accounts, but you can freeze them so that further debts are not incurred with them.

While you technically are likely not liable for debts incurred by your spouse after you separate, you will still have to deal with creditors coming to you for payment if your spouse does not pay. Further, delayed payments on your joint accounts will likely be reported to the credit rating agencies, making it harder for you to secure a loan or credit card in the future. It may be suggested that you simply remove your name from an account rather than close it. Be careful though; people who have been removed have still been chased by creditors in nonpayment situations, whether this is legitimate or not.

If you are a financially dependent spouse, you will most often want to open an individual account at the time you close a joint one. If your credit has been based on your spouse's earnings, you will want to begin establishing credit in your own name. It may be difficult to establish your own credit if you do not yet have income. One way to begin is with a credit card secured with a deposit at your bank. Research your options in this area and make sure you deal with reputable firms. There are a number of unscrupulous companies operating in the credit repair arena. Some institutions offer secured cards that can be converted to credit accounts after some period of time.

Of course, joint checking and savings accounts need to be dealt with if they have any significant funds in them or are backed with a credit line. You can cut off access to such credit as you would with a credit card. And again, you may want to go ahead and open an individual account in your own name. You may transfer up to half of the funds in your joint accounts to your individual account. However, do not leave either account in such a position that checks will bounce and the accounts will incur new fees as you incur new headaches.

Review your financial information to identify bills for things such as utilities that are in your name. If, as a result of moving out, you are no longer using for instance, electricity or telephone—or your spouse's cell phone is in your name—you will want to modify the payment arrangements. It may be difficult to get your spouse to pay these bills or to reimburse you.

There are more complex protective actions that may be warranted in some situations. A lawyer may also be able to protect the assets of your marriage through an injunction restraining your spouse from transferring or otherwise disposing of any property covered by the restraining order. There may also be property in your spouse's possession that will not be considered as part of your property distribution. Your attorney might also be able to use an injunction to get that property returned to you prior to the resolution of other issues in your divorce.

Although rarely used, another self-protective step is to file with a court what is known as a *lis pendens* in the deeds office of any county where you or your spouse or both of you own real property. The lis pendens puts third parties on notice of your claim to have an interest in the real estate against which the lis pendens is docketed. The lis pendens is basically a notice of pending litigation that may affect real property. A properly recorded and served lis pendens clouds the title to the property, preventing an effective sale of the property behind your back.

Finally, you should consider what might happen if you die before your divorce is finalized. You may talk with a family law attorney or an attorney with expertise in estate planning about your options regarding insurance and assets. These professionals can advise you about whether it is possible, and whether it makes sense, to change the beneficiaries on any insurance policies you own. You might also consider changing the way your property is titled. It is most likely that your home is held in what is called *joint tenancy*. In this situation, if one spouse dies, the property transfers to the other spouse, regardless of what is in the deceased party's will. *Tenancy in common* is different. Your interest in property held this way is yours alone. It transfers according to wishes you stated in your will. In most states, an owner of a property held with joint tenancy may modify the ownership to tenancy in common by filing a statement with the deeds office, even without their spouse's consent. However, just because it is possible does not mean it is advisable.

---

# Documenting Your Net Worth

Once you have gathered all of your financial information and have taken steps to protect your finances during the divorce process, you need to prepare for your negotiations by documenting your net worth and preparing a budget for life after divorce. We will deal with net worth first.

To determine your net worth, you add all of your assets together. You do the same for your debts, or liabilities. You subtract your debts from your assets to get your total net worth. After having read through the information above, you should be familiar with your assets. You will likely need to research or perform appraisals to get accurate values for at least some of your possessions. For others, particularly pension plans, you will want help from a CPA or other financial professional. When you have these numbers, or near estimates, make a list and total them. If you would like to use a worksheet as a starting point, just look for one online.

Why do you need to go through this exercise? Clearly, the more informed you are about your finances, the better decisions you will make during negotiations. Also, you may learn that when you put everything together, you have far more—or less—than you imagined. This can influence your strategy in negotiations. If you and your spouse have a total net worth of $25,000 and you each make significant use of lawyers, and possibly a mediator, to help you agree about how to divide your property, the fees you pay could easily outweigh any gains you might achieve beyond your spouse's initial offer. Alternatively, if you find that the net worth is greater than you thought, you may decide that it is worth more effort, and potentially fees, to ensure you receive a fair amount.

## Budgeting for Life after Divorce

Your net worth indicates your *current* financial picture. A budget is meant to help you predict your *future* needs. Your budget will be critically important for setting expectations about what you can afford as well as negotiating any support payments. Realize that you will likely need to continually modify your budget as you go through negotiations.

You and your spouse should develop budgets independently. The only way to develop a realistic budget is to review your actual past spending. Your initial budget should show what it takes to maintain your current lifestyle. Depending on your situation, you may need to squeeze your budget later. For now, go through the records you have collected and ensure that you are including all that you have spent. Again, you may find an online worksheet to be enormously helpful.

If you are computer savvy, a copy of Intuit's Quicken or Microsoft's Money can help you create your budget and then track your progress as you go through your separation to make sure your numbers are realistic.

If you have children, a useful next step is to identify how much of each item in your budget is attributable to your children. Be fair when doing this, though. For instance, if you have two children, you cannot reasonably say that two-thirds of your car expenses are attributable to your children, since you would most likely still need a car without them. However, if you are driving a larger car, or more importantly, living in a larger house or apartment because the children live with you, it is reasonable to identify that difference. At this time, you may not be certain about the children's living arrangements, so you may need to prepare versions of your budget for a couple of scenarios.

Having information from both parents about the costs that will be incurred as a result of caring for the children will be helpful when you negotiate child support. It is often the case that the spouse who is making the child support payments is concerned the money is going to support things other than the children. Having a clear budget that you can review and discuss can head off much of this conflict.

Your budgeting to this point has most likely focused on expenses. You will also need to calculate your post-divorce income. Your expenses are usually paid with after-tax income, so you will need to know how much you're actually bringing home each month. Your divorce will affect the amount you pay in taxes as a result of several factors: a change in tax filing status from married to single, the way you agree to handle exemptions for dependents, and whether you end up with a home loan whose interest you can deduct. Although you may not initially know the details of how exemptions and real estate will be handled, as you move through the process, you need to keep an eye on your post-divorce tax situation, as it could significantly affect your ability to balance your budget.

When you and your spouse review each other's budgets, you may find that your combined income is less than your expenses. If this is the case, you will need to take some time to review the situation. Control your urge to critique your spouse's expenses, as that can easily inflame the situation. You may both need to reduce expenses, but it is better to focus on your own budget, because you are the best one to decide what is important to you.

Your budgets will be critical in negotiating any alimony or child support. It can be hard work to prepare an initial budget. However, it cannot be avoided if you are to have confidence and maintain control over the outcome of your divorce. In fact, you will most likely need several versions of your budget, preferably prepared in advance, that take into account various possibilities, such as the effect of selling your home (and the new housing expenses you incur), the effect of going back to work (and the new child care expenses that might result), and other possibilities that might be up for discussion as you and your spouse work to reach agreement.

## The Cost of Divorce

As you have probably already guessed, the advice of an attorney comes with a price tag. The final number on that price tag is going to be influenced by a lot of factors, only some of which you can control. As we pointed out earlier, you can assume that your fees will total somewhere between $5,000 and $30,000. That's a pretty wide range—there are many variables.

The bottom-line figure that you will ultimately shell out to your attorney will most likely be a composite number, including more than just the cost of legal representation. For every expert who is called in to analyze your case or testify on your behalf, there will be a fee, which will show up in the bills from your attorney. Your bill will also reflect the complexity or difficulty of your case, as well as the general atmosphere between yourself and your spouse. Settling before the case goes to court is much less expensive than not reaching an amicable agreement.

There are some other factors, which are much more subtle and thus harder to identify, that will impact your attorney fees. Obviously, in some parts of the country, lawyers have no choice but to charge rates that are commensurate with a locally higher standard of living. Similarly, there are sometimes differences in fees charged by urban versus suburban lawyers. Hiring a board-certified family-law specialist, which can be very helpful in a more complicated case, can cost a good deal more than hiring a general practitioner.

Some attorneys have alternative fee structures or payment plans that may or may not result in a better financial deal for certain types of clients. A flat fee, for instance, may be an excellent plan for someone whose case is likely to necessitate business valuations, real estate appraisals, and a psychologist, but a young couple with no kids and few assets may be better off paying the hourly fees and coming to a quick resolution. When you are shopping around for an attorney, consider how each attorney structures the billing system as well as the payment arrangements, and hold out for the plan that works best for you.

---

# Making Smart Financial Decisions

We have said it before: divorce is an emotional, legal, and financial process. Your best strategy is to focus most of your energy on the financial issues while reducing the influence of emotion and following the rules set out by the law. As you move through the divorce process, you will need to make many financial decisions. Follow these guidelines to make the best decisions possible.

***Avoid the temptation to take a vacation from financial reality.*** We have seen people spend more money than they should when their marriage is ending because they feel great, feel depressed, or think that somehow their spouse will wind up with the bill. While it may be hard to accept, divorce is likely to change your lifestyle in such a way that you have to be more careful with money than you were before—even if you were a penny pincher. The sooner you accept this change and begin conserving your financial resources, the better off you will be.

***Value your property as if you were selling it.*** As you consider the value of items during negotiations, do more than just consider the item's market value. This is particularly true when dealing with a house, where you can wind up paying 5 percent of the sale price, or more, to real estate agents if you want, or need, to sell it. It is common for people who initially think they will stay in the marital home for many years after divorce to sell it in a much shorter period. Such moves are hard to predict, but the costs associated with selling a property are easier to know and should be taken into account.

*Do not forget about taxes.* Lawyers generally have a basic understanding of tax implications for common situations. However, you may need to talk to an accountant if you have anything that is nonstandard. One example of a tax implication you might overlook is when an investment account is divided. Stocks in the account may have different amounts of taxable capital gains. If you don't take that into account when valuing them, you could be at risk of getting less than you expect.

*Choose cash now.* When negotiating the property division or alimony portions of your divorce agreement, you may be given the option of receiving payments for a specified period of time or receiving a lump-sum immediately. The lump sum would be less money than if you added up the ongoing payments. However, you need to consider three things when contemplating a decision like this. First, money you receive in the future will be worth less than an equal amount of money you receive today, as a result of inflation. Second, money you have today has more value to you because you can benefit from investing it. Third, if you get an immediate payment, you do not have the risk that your spouse will fail to make the promised future payments. When we take these factors into account, in most cases, we advise people to take the lump sum, even though it may be a smaller amount. This same rule applies to other types of promises of future compensation.

*Adapt to changed circumstances quickly.* Trying to hold onto a lifestyle that is no longer affordable can cause you to get into significant debt faster than you might think. You will need to monitor monthly expenses carefully to ensure that the budgets you created during the divorce process were realistic. If you find otherwise, you need to take an honest look at whether what you are seeing are unusual expenses, perhaps related to setting up a new residence, or expenses that you can expect will recur and will need to be cut or eliminated.

*Do not make quick decisions about major commitments.* If at the beginning of your divorce, you owned a home with your spouse, and you now find yourself selling or moving out of that house, be wary of the urge to make a new major commitment quickly. Not only may you find that your post-divorce budget won't support the home you want but you may also find that within a few months of your divorce you have very different feelings about your needs. Your life is going through a major change, and it is difficult to predict exactly how things will turn out. As a result, you should use caution and consider renting or some other short-term option that allows you some time to get through the adjustment before taking on significant debt or long-term financial obligations.

*Consider the cost of the fight.* We write a lot about avoiding court fights. It's also important to realize that even if you avoid going to court, you can easily run up large attorney fees. It's not extraordinary for complex cases going to court to cost the marital estate hundreds of thousands of dollars. All too often people spend more in fees and their own time arguing about a particularly emotional piece of personal property than the item is actually worth. Try to remove emotion as much as possible from your negotiations and think like a business person. Always review whether the cost of winning the fight is worth the reward. Ultimately, the ability to step back from strong feelings and make a calm, rational decision is one of the most valuable life skills that you can hone during your divorce.

---

# Getting Extra Help

We run across many people who are not comfortable dealing with finances, primarily because the other spouse handled things for many years. If you are in this situation, you will at least want to learn the basics so you can make informed decisions during divorce. However, you may have too much going on in your life right now to learn everything you need to know. There is a whole industry of professionals who are willing and able to help you with your finances, and it can be a good idea to get some help. Even those who are used to managing day-to-day finances for the household will want some help in dealing with complex issues such as valuing pension plans or family businesses.

The types of financial professionals that can help people going through divorce include accountants (CPA), business valuation experts, and financial planners. Accountants are used in at least two ways. If one of the assets to be dealt with in your divorce is a business, you may need the help of an accountant to review the business records as part of the valuation process. Such a review may help to identify unusual activity intended to deceive you or the government regarding the state of the business. Accountants also help evaluate the tax consequence of various options that you may be considering as part of your settlement negotiations.

If it looks as though your case is going to trial, and either you or your spouse owns a business, then you will need to hire business valuation experts who will testify. If you are going to settle the case without going to court, then your need for an expert will depend on the type of business being divided. Engage people at varying levels—sometimes a quick and dirty analysis, conducted for a small fee, can be used just for negotiations so that you don't need to obtain a full-fledged report that an expert would draw up when preparing to give testimony.

Business brokers have day-to-day information on selling businesses. If the business in question is in a highly technical or specialized field, it may be necessary to hire an expert from within that industry. In reality, an expert is anybody who can provide helpful information to the court, so you have to think about where you can find the right people for the case.

Unless you have a relationship with an accountant or business valuation expert, we recommend getting referrals from any attorney or mediator you are working with. Using someone they refer you to helps ensure they can work well together. If you are in an adversarial situation, it is likely that you and your spouse will each have your own experts. If you wind up in court, a judge may even bring in a third, neutral expert. This is the most costly way to do things. If possible, invest time in working to get your spouse to agree to use a single expert at the outset.

Financial planners are primarily helpful when it comes to educating people. If you have never managed your own (or your family's) finances, then you may want to consider enlisting the services of a financial planner. The one caveat is if your situation is particularly complicated—if you need sophisticated tax advice, for instance—you would be better off consulting a CPA or tax lawyer. When choosing a financial planner, look for one who is independent. There are many financial planners out there, but often they work for a particular company that is tied to certain investments or insurance. In general, you are better off with independent firms or individuals that have access to a variety of funds and insurance companies. When in doubt, ask about the variety of their resources.

The divorce process alters most people's financial plans significantly. In some cases, people end up with assets that their spouses had previously managed. The spouse acquiring the assets may need assistance in determining how best to manage them. On the other hand, if you are losing assets or part of your income stream, you may need assistance recreating savings plans for retirement or education. This is the domain of financial planners. They can help you determine your net worth, create budgets, manage investments, analyze insurance needs, monitor the results of your plans, and update them as warranted.

Some financial planners now specialize in helping people going through divorce. Rather than simply helping you plan your post-divorce finances, these professionals are involved in the divorce process from the beginning. They can help you with all of the work involved in preparing for negotiations, including preparing the statement of net worth, as well as those realistic budgets. They can help with the creation and evaluation of the financial aspects of settlement proposals. And of course, a financial planner will be happy to help you manage your money after the divorce. An expert focused on these areas may be able to save you money in your divorce by decreasing your legal fees. Just as you do not want to use a lawyer as a therapist, you want to be cautious about relying exclusively on a lawyer for financial advice. Divorce attorneys should have good financial backgrounds, but not all do.

# Divorce Law

The prior two chapters focused on the emotional and financial aspects of divorce. Of course, there are also legal issues that you need to be aware of as you go through the process. If you are able to stay out of court, then you will have a lot less legal bureaucracy to deal with. In this chapter, we review the basics of divorce law to help you make wise decisions and avoid any legal missteps. Future chapters will delve deeper into the law, as it relates to property division, alimony, child custody, and child support.

## What Is a Divorce?

Divorce is the legal dissolution of marriage. When you divorce, a court changes your legal status so that the rights and obligations you obtained when you got married are removed. These rights include tax benefits (filing joint return), estate planning benefits (inheriting part of spouse's estate), and employment benefits (family participation in group health plan). The primary obligation removed by divorce is the need to maintain sexual fidelity. It is important to keep in mind that these rights and obligations are not removed *until the divorce is final.* This raises a number of questions about your conduct during separation. We will address those in the next chapter, "Life During Divorce."

## Divorce Is a State Issue

State, not federal, laws regulate marriage and divorce. The federal government provides certain rights to married people, including the right to have your marriage recognized in any state. However, as of the initial publication of this book, they have mostly stayed out of marriage and divorce. The lack of federal involvement means there are differences in the way divorce is handled in each state. Even so, the states have generally coalesced around two or three ways of handling the matters relating to divorce.

As we cover the basics of divorce law, we will highlight the areas you will need to learn about in your particular state. In this do-it-yourself era, you may be tempted to read through your state's family law statutes online or in a library to get these details. We applaud any effort to become more educated about divorce. One place where you can find a great deal of state-specific information about divorce laws is Divorce Source's state divorce laws section.

Another online source for state-specific information is your state court's website. You can locate the site by doing an Internet search for the name of your state followed by "courts". For instance, "Maryland courts" shows the Maryland Judiciary site as the first result. Once you locate the website for your state's courts look for "divorce," frequently asked questions (FAQ), or a self-help center. In most cases you will find the state-specific process information you need.

An important thing to keep in mind when reading your state's laws is that the law's text is only part of the story. For simple situations, the statutes are likely to provide understandable wording that is interpreted in court as you would expect. But in more complex circumstances, judges resolve conflicts in the law or determine how to handle situations that lawmakers did not explicitly address. It is usually necessary to work with a lawyer to understand the relevance of any prior court decisions to your divorce. Aside from knowing about many legal principles, a local family law attorney will be, or should be, familiar with these judicial opinions.

## Legal Separation

Some states have a concept of legal separation. In those states, couples who want to stay married for religious reasons may opt for legal separation instead of divorce. Others become legally separated because courts address legal separations faster than divorces. In those areas of the country, legal separation can be a solution for couples who are unable to negotiate the divorce issues or have yet to meet the residency requirements but require a separation agreement for financial or other reasons. Becoming legally separated usually requires a court order or separation agreement addressing the same issues that are covered in divorce agreements. The laws around legal separation vary from state to state. In some states you can only become legally separated as part of the divorce process, but others allow you to remain legally separated indefinitely.

---

# Residency Requirements

It is common for people to believe that they need to get divorced in the state in which they were married. Fortunately, given the mobility of our society, this is not the case. You generally get divorced where you currently live. The person filing for divorce must be a resident of the state. A few states have no minimum length of time that you must have been a resident prior to seeking a divorce, so you could file for divorce on the same day you arrive in the state. Other states require anywhere from six weeks to one year of residency prior to filing for divorce. The most common time period is six months. It is not uncommon for one spouse to move to a different state at the time of separation. In this case, there may be a choice as to where the divorce can be filed.

If you find that you want or need to file for divorce, or respond to such a filing, in a state other than where you live, you will want to find a local (meaning in the state of which you are *not* a resident) attorney to represent you. If you don't have contacts there you can count on for a referral, you can consult legal networks or website directories for more information

If there are custody or property issues or both, however, the filing rules are slightly different. There is a uniform law that has been adopted by all states that deals with custody and property: generally people have to file in the state where the kids live and have been for six months. This helps with availability of witnesses. The same is true for property division; usually those cases are filed in the state where the property is located. There is a different uniform law that deals with child support, and it is a little more complicated.

---

# Fault vs. No-Fault

Prior to what some have dubbed "the divorce revolution" that began in the 1970s, marriage was treated similarly to a contract. To get a divorce, you had to prove your spouse was at fault in breaking the marital contract. Things such as infidelity, drug addiction, desertion, and impotence qualified as valid reasons. Claiming and proving these faults was often embarrassing and costly. If a married person simply wanted to end the marriage because of unhappiness, they would either be stuck or have to lie. This approach did not take into account the complexity of marital relationships. In most cases, the failure of the marriage is not the fault of one spouse alone.

Today's laws are quite different with regard to fault. Every state offers spouses a way to become divorced without assigning fault to one spouse. Even so, you still need to provide a reason, or what is known as a ground, for the divorce. The grounds are, however, usually vague and no longer require parties to blame one another for the end of the marriage.

There are two major types of no-fault divorce. The first allows you to simply claim that you and your spouse are incompatible—that you have irreconcilable differences—or that there has been an irremediable breakdown of the marriage. About fifteen states include these types of grounds for divorce. The rest of the states require you to live separate and apart from your spouse for some period of time, ranging from sixty days to two years. The legal definition of separation varies, with some states requiring separate residences and others allowing couples to live in the same house but not share sex. In some states, it is not necessary to have been separated prior to the *filing* of the divorce, but the divorce is only *granted* after the required period of separation.

Although no-fault divorce grounds are available in all states, more than half the states also allow you or your spouse to claim fault in your divorce. The grounds available vary, but abandonment and infidelity/adultery are standard. If you live in a state that allows for fault-based divorce and you feel you are able to prove your spouse is at fault for the divorce (based on the fault grounds available in your state), the question becomes: Does it make sense for you to file for divorce using one of the grounds? In about half of the states, a finding of fault could affect alimony, so if you are in a position where you might be liable for such payments, you might consider such a claim in order to avoid paying. A small number of states go so far as to disqualify a spouse from receiving alimony if he or she is found at fault. Fault also is a factor in property division in nearly half the states.

Although bringing fault into your divorce could work to your advantage in some states, you need to review your goals for your divorce, the potential costs of proving fault, and the likely benefits to be gained if you succeed. It is important to remember that most divorces are settled without going to court. However, when you claim fault, or your spouse does, legal fees for both of you are likely to rise dramatically, because rather than solely focusing on negotiating your divorce agreement, your attorneys must also work to prove the fault claim. Your spouse's fees will also rise as he or she prepares to defend against the claim. The net result is a decrease in your marital property, which in many cases, may exceed the benefit you could win in the fight.

Although the influence of fault on judges has diminished greatly in the past twenty years, the claim is certain to affect your negotiations with your spouse. A claim of fault creates a higher degree of uncertainty. People involved in negotiations where the alternative to an agreement is highly uncertain have an incentive to come to agreement in order to obtain a sense of certainty—it's sort of a "devil you don't know is worse than the devil you do know" kind of scenario.

The decision of whether to include a claim of fault in your divorce filing is something to discuss with a lawyer familiar with your state's laws and the potential outcomes you might achieve if you end up in court. In doing so, remember that that your lawyer may have some bias in the matter if he or she stands to earn large fees from representing you in a more complex divorce. You need to analyze the amount you stand to gain, the likelihood of achieving that outcome, and the cost of the fight before making a decision. You also need to remember that the decision is yours to make. Take advice from your attorney, but be sure you do not give up control of your divorce.

---

# Proving Fault

If you decide to introduce one or more claims of fault into your divorce, you will need to gather evidence to support the claims. Faults such as abandonment can be difficult to prove. In North Carolina, for instance, abandonment is defined as leaving the marriage without just cause or without consent, and in some states (North Carolina included), abandonment applies only to alimony judgments, not to the divorce itself.

Adultery is another type of fault that must be proven. When it is necessary to prove an adulterous relationship, you may consider the use of a private investigator, a review of phone records, recording of phone calls, and a search of a computer. At our law firm, we have good working relationships with several private investigators that do surveillance and lawful forensic work with computers. We compile records of cell phone usage and more. We examine credit card records and other records, looking for evidence of some kind of fault. If there is an accusation of physical abuse, we use photographs, medical records, and other documentation. We can sometimes even subpoena travel records from an employer.

A word to the wise: sometimes it's prudent to gather the information early to have it in case you need it, but that doesn't necessarily mean you have to go in that direction.

---

# Uncontested Divorce

Almost all divorces are uncontested, which means the parties were able to work out the issues of the divorce without the assistance of the court. Even though the parties have agreed in advance, a divorce is a legal action that involves the filing of a civil case. The spouse who filed the divorce complaint, or that person's lawyer, may be required to appear in court. This appearance usually involves a judge reviewing the agreement between you and your spouse and asking a few questions to confirm the information you have supplied. The other situation that warrants an uncontested divorce is one in which one spouse fails to file a response to the complaint or to appear in court.

Although the inclusion of fault grounds in a divorce complaint can lead to a bitterly contested divorce, filing for a no-fault divorce does not mean the divorce will be uncontested. Even in a no-fault divorce, you and your spouse may be unable to agree on the divorce issues, which would result in a judge resolving them for you. Likewise, a divorce that includes fault grounds could conceivably be resolved without a judge.

# Divorce Procedure

Although this book is about divorce, getting your actual legal divorce is usually the easiest part of the process. That is, if you successfully negotiate all of the financial and child-related issues with your spouse, your hard work is done. Getting the legal divorce is essentially a bureaucratic process.

As with getting married, getting a divorce requires completing a legal procedure mandated by your state. Regardless of whether you and your spouse have already agreed on the financial and child-related issues, every state requires you to file a divorce complaint or petition with the court. This complaint is the beginning of a civil lawsuit. The spouse who files the complaint or petition becomes the plaintiff, or petitioner, in the case. The other spouse is referred to as the defendant, or respondent.

The timing of filing your divorce complaint is dependent on your state, the grounds you choose to include, and whether you are in need of temporary alimony or child support. For instance, in order to obtain a no-fault divorce, some states require a period of separation prior to filing. In others, a required period of separation begins at the time of filing. A filing with fault grounds may have no such waiting periods in your state but, of course, may take longer in the end if your spouse chooses to contest the filing.

One concern we often hear from clients is how they will manage their financial details during the limbo-like period of separation. Most states have laws in place that provide stop-gap measures to ensure that children, particularly, are taken care of during the upheaval of a divorce. Federal laws mandate that states move quickly on child support issues. In North Carolina, for instance, a request for temporary child support could be the first issue filed in a case. Nothing would have to precede it—you could even still be living together. An attorney will be able to explain the details in your state, but systems are in place to ensure the relatively smooth division of one household into two.

Another issue to consider with regard to *when* you begin the legal divorce proceeding is where you are in the emotional process of ending your marriage. It is important, at some point, to go ahead and start the clock running. But generally, the more easily a couple can talk about their plans before starting anything that feels like an adversarial process, the less likely it is that things will blow up on them. It would not be good for your spouse to be surprised by having a police officer serve him or her with divorce papers.

As you consider filing for divorce, you may wonder if it makes a difference whether you or your spouse files first. In most cases, the spouse who files first does not receive any significant advantage. The filing spouse is able to withdraw the divorce case if he or she has a change of heart, whereas the nonfiling spouse could not do so unilaterally. If the nonfiling spouse did not want the divorce but the filing spouse did, a divorce based on no-fault grounds would be granted even over the nonfiling spouse's objection.

Once a divorce complaint is filed, you or your attorney must formally notify your spouse. This is known as serving the papers on your spouse. In some jurisdictions, you may be able to serve the papers by certified mail, although the state may require that someone other than you send the mail. Service can be handled by a sheriff or, if your spouse is attempting to evade service, by a private process server. It is often possible for your spouse to sign a document that waives the need to serve the divorce papers on him or her. This method is common in uncontested divorces or when both parties have lawyers representing them, thus eliminating the potential embarrassment of a sheriff arriving to serve papers at someone's workplace.

Once the papers are served, the nonfiling spouse (defendant) has a limited period of time (twenty to sixty days) in which to file a response. In uncontested situations, the defendant may choose to not file a response. If you are the defendant and choose to not file a response the judge may award all of the requests in the divorce complaint. Filing a response allows you to let the court and your spouse know what items in the complaint you agree or disagree with. If you have yet to come to agreement on the divorce issues, your response will be part of stating your position in your negotiations. If you receive a response, check it carefully to ensure that your spouse has indicated agreement with everything in the complaint. If you were expecting an uncontested divorce and were handling things without a lawyer, a response contesting items in your divorce complaint should give you pause and prompt you to at least consult with a lawyer so that you understand your legal options.

Because divorce involves the division of property and, potentially, alimony, some states require you to complete a financial disclosure or affidavit. You may need to file this information with the court or serve it on your spouse or both. This helps ensure that everyone is aware of all financial details prior to the dissolution of the marriage, after which it may be difficult or impossible to address any inequity.

In an uncontested divorce—once the divorce complaint, response, and any required financial forms are complete—the spouse who filed the complaint, or his or her attorney, will need to complete some additional forms to prepare for the finalization of the divorce. This will include a divorce judgment that the judge will review and, if all is proper, sign.

In some states, there is a required period of separation between the filing and the granting of the divorce. In others, if you have met the requirements (one of which may be a period of separation), the court will hear your case fairly quickly (thirty to sixty days). When the date comes for your divorce to be reviewed by a judge, you or your attorney may need to appear in court. If everything is in order, the judge will sign your divorce judgment or decree. In order to truly finalize the divorce, the filing party or their attorney may be required to file this document and serve it on their spouse.

# Simplified Procedures

Contested divorces are the most complex type of divorce. Uncontested divorces are easier but still usually require a court appearance. Some states have streamlined the uncontested divorce further and offer what are known as simplified divorces, or summary dissolutions. These are generally available only to people who have a fairly short marriage (less than five or ten years), have no children, have limited property and debts, will not require alimony, and meet other restrictions. The process usually reduces the amount and complexity of paperwork involved.

In some states, the simplified procedure eliminates the need for a court hearing, whereas in others it requires that both parties be present in court. An important difference you need to be aware of when considering the use of a simplified procedure, which does not involve a court hearing, is that if a judge makes a decision you are dissatisfied with, you do not have the standard ability to ask for a new trial or appeal. There will likely be other alternatives, but they can be expensive, time consuming, and difficult. Unless one spouse has hidden a large asset or income stream, the cost of a standard appeal would usually be greater than the reward for couples who meet the requirements for the simplified procedure.

# Military Divorce

Divorces involving people currently in the military or those with military pensions are more complex than others. This is an area where federal law comes into the divorce process. Some of the differences include residency requirements, the manner in which divorce papers must be served on a spouse on active duty, and the way a military pension is divided. We recommend that even if you choose not to use an attorney in your negotiations, you consult an experienced family law attorney to get a deeper understanding of how your or your spouse's association with the military will affect your divorce.

# Using Your Maiden Name

If you changed your name at the time of your marriage and you want to return to using your maiden name, you are usually free to do so. It is generally unnecessary to go to court to get the name change, but procedures vary widely from state to state. In some states, you have the option of changing your name as part of your divorce. In others you simply need to notify government agencies that have records of you name, including the IRS and your state taxing authorities; the Social Security Administration; the post office; your driver's license bureau; and the companies you have relationships with, including your bank, credit card companies, and other lenders. It can be useful to have the divorce decree state that you will resume your unmarried name, but generally it is not necessary to do so to have a valid name change.

# Alienation of Affection and Criminal Conversation

Seven states—Hawaii, Illinois, Mississippi, New Mexico, North Carolina, South Dakota, and Utah—have laws allowing a spouse to sue for damages based on allegations of emotional harm caused by a third party to the marital relationship. These lawsuits for "alienation of affection" and/or "criminal conversation" are usually brought by the innocent spouse against the guilty spouse's lover. A case might also be brought against an in-law or other near relative who advised a defecting spouse to leave the marriage. The laws vary greatly between the states, and the suits can be complex, requiring jury trials. However, sometimes the costs may be worth it, as recent cases in North Carolina have resulted in jury awards of hundreds of thousands of dollars. Some cases result in an award of over one million dollars. The possibility of such a massive judgment can create great incentive for a spouse involved in an adulterous relationship to settle to avoid potential damage to a person outside of the marriage with whom they have a relationship.

---

# Covenant Divorce

In reaction to the no-fault divorce movement that made divorce easier, Arizona, Arkansas, and Louisiana have passed laws that allow couples to choose what is termed a "covenant marriage." Couples who choose a covenant marriage voluntarily make it more difficult to become divorced, especially without fault. In general, the period of separation required for ending a covenant marriage is at least double that required for standard divorces. As part of getting a covenant marriage, couples attend premarital counseling on the "nature, purposes, and responsibilities of marriage,"[10] and agree to seek further counseling during any marital difficulties.

---

# Annulments

An annulment (or "nullity of marriage") is when a court says your marriage is not legally valid. A marriage that is incestuous or bigamous is never valid. In general, marriages can be declared "void" because:

- Of force, fraud, or physical or mental incapacity
- One of the spouses was too young to legally marry
- One of the spouses was already married

Some states also allow annulments if the marriage was performed under the belief that the wife was pregnant, and if certain other restrictions are met. Although it is not uncommon for people to ask about them, annulments are very rare. The problem with annulment is that if a marriage is declared invalid, then certain protections that would be provided by the divorce process (such as the extension of COBRA health benefits) are removed. If you think one of these criteria is applicable to your situation, then you should consider the option of annulment very carefully, preferably in consultation with a divorce lawyer.

# Notes

[10] Arizona Revised Statutes, *Marital and Domestic Relations*, § 25-901 (B)(1)(A).
http://www.azleg.gov/FormatDocument.asp?inDoc=/ars/25/00901.htm &Title=25&DocType=ARS.

# Working with A Lawyer

Americans have a generally disdainful view of lawyers. Research by the American Bar Association has shown that many people believe lawyers fail to make divorce simpler and less painful. Being lawyers, we find this disheartening but somewhat understandable. In this chapter, we will discuss what drives the perception that lawyers are not helpful, how to determine if a lawyer can help you in your divorce, and how to find a lawyer you will like if you decide you need one.

The do-it-yourself divorce, or what we often call the kitchen-table approach, has become increasingly popular, especially since the Internet made it easier for people to find information and tools to assist them. The do-it-yourself trend, along with other factors, has caused lawyers to reconsider how they offer their services. In the past, a lawyer may have only worked on your divorce if he or she was going to work on every aspect of it. Today, attorneys are more willing to assist in very specific ways and allow you to handle part of the work. In this chapter, we will consider the benefits and risks of working with a lawyer in this way.

## Why Do People Dislike Lawyers?

If you come to divorce with some trepidation about involving a lawyer, you are not alone. Our experience is that people perceive that lawyers add conflict to situations. This feeling, combined with the perceived expense of hiring a lawyer, is a large part of why people dislike lawyers. You may be surprised to find that we agree with much of the criticism levied against lawyers.

To be helpful in divorce cases, lawyers have to overcome a couple of inherent obstacles. First, the types of people who choose to go to law school are usually cautious and averse to risk. Second, once in law school, those people are trained to become part of the adversarial American legal system, in which lawyers work as zealous advocates for their clients. These seem like positive things, but they can cause problems when it comes to handling divorce cases.

It is rare that divorce cases go, or should go, to court. Because almost all cases end with a negotiated settlement, a lawyer's primary mission in a divorce *should be* to help negotiate a reasonable settlement. However, an overly cautious lawyer may regard an offer from one spouse as full of potential problems and may work to address every possible future scenario, regardless of how unlikely it may be. Great care is necessary in creating a comprehensive agreement, but going overboard by raising red flags about every inconsequential detail can lead to a drawn-out process. This raises the risk of one spouse becoming frustrated and losing the desire to settle. It is often the case that there is a time when everyone is very close to agreement. A lawyer who fails to seize such opportunities because of some imperfections in the agreement can cause a case to cost more and be more contentious than necessary.

Lawyers who, partly as a result of their training, view every case as a fight also contribute to the notion that lawyers do more harm than good. They focus their efforts on finding ways to attack their adversary rather than looking for common ground between the parties. A lawyer who focuses on being an adversary will generally drive spouses further apart. This approach is counterproductive, as it lengthens the amount of time it takes for the parties to come together and agree on the major issues in their divorce. In families in which the on-going parenting of children is involved, a lawyer who unnecessarily increases the rancor in the relationship can do damage that can be difficult to repair.

Our final critique of lawyers has to do with their definition of success in divorce cases. As we said, lawyers are trained to be zealous advocates for their clients. They want to get as much as they can for them. The problem arises in how you measure things. Lawyers tend to focus on tangible items, particularly money. The more of the marital estate they secure for their client, the more successful they feel. However, there are other factors that are less tangible but still very important. Our experience is that clients do not measure the "success" of their divorce solely by the dollars they receive, but by how they feel at the end of the process. It is useful for lawyers to remind their clients not to be overly emotional in their negotiations. However, we think lawyers who treat divorce solely as a business transaction and ignore the emotional piece of the picture end up with clients who are dissatisfied with the results.

## Do You Need a Lawyer?

The question of whether you need a lawyer comes down to how much you have at risk in your divorce and how much time you have. If you and your spouse have very few assets, comparable incomes, and no children, you have little to lose in handling your divorce in a do-it-yourself manner, without the assistance of an attorney. You might even choose to work solely with a mediator to help you in the process of working out all the necessary details and creating the settlement agreement. Reviewing our chapter "Divorce and Finances" will help ensure that you have considered all of the assets that might be considered marital property. You may be a renter without much money in the bank but may have life insurance, retirement plans, or other assets that may not be immediately obvious to you. It is critical that you fully evaluate your financial picture if you are considering moving forward without the help of a lawyer.

A lawyer plays several roles in divorce: information provider, negotiator, advisor, and implementer. First, lawyers provide information that is not easily obtained. For instance, even in relatively simple situations, dividing property can involve legal questions. In particular, it can be difficult to identify the property that should be treated as separate property and what belongs to both of you. A lawyer can help with these determinations, so you know what you would be entitled to if the case went to court.

The range of information a lawyer can provide about handling your divorce is broad and includes issues relating to how the timing of your divorce can affect you financially. For example, you might not know that you must be married for at least ten years in order to qualify for social security spousal benefits, or that if you wait until you are fifty-five to sell the marital residence, you get a tax break. The financial impact of just having access to such information can be highly significant. You might be able to search the Internet and find the facts a lawyer would provide, but the time spent and the difficulty in ensuring that the information is accurate and relevant to your situation usually mean that it is worthwhile to talk to an expert who has most of the information you might need readily accessible.

Many people feel that they have trouble negotiating a good deal. This is even the case when they are trying to buy something, which is a situation in which they should have a great deal of power. Negotiating with a spouse can be much more difficult, especially when one or both of you find it hard to avoid rehashing what has happened in your relationship rather than focusing on the present and future. Another challenge occurs when one spouse is controlling.

Easing the difficulty people have in negotiations is one thing lawyers do well. They are less emotionally vested in a situation and therefore can view things more objectively. Lawyers also undergo training in negotiating strategies that enable them to avoid falling into traps; they can thus greatly reduce the time required to reach agreement. The fact that they are constantly involved in negotiations puts lawyers at ease when they are negotiating. That alone can increase the effectiveness of a negotiator. The bottom line is that if you are not comfortable with or skilled in negotiations, a lawyer's help can be of great value.

A third role lawyers play is that of advisor. An experienced family law attorney will understand issues that you haven't even thought of yet, and will be able to direct you to resources that might even help you avoid some common pitfalls. Have you gotten mental health support for your kids yet? Have you considered hiring a financial planner to help you work out a budget that you can stick to after you've separated? Have you considered talking to an accountant about the potential tax implications of liquidating your assets in order to divide them? While divorce lawyers obviously can't specialize in that wide a range of issues, their experience is broad enough that they can often anticipate the problems before you can, and can advise you on where to go for help. And while we are certainly not trained therapists, most divorce lawyers will tell you that a large part of what they do every day resembles therapy—helping our clients sort through the emotional muddle and get back on their feet. A lawyer can also advise you if an unexpected problem comes up—for instance, if your spouse files for bankruptcy before you receive money due to you in a property settlement. A lawyer may be able to help you notify your spouse about the divorce if you are unable to do so. Additionally, a lawyer can advise you on how much money, if any, you should pay or receive for alimony or child support.

Finally, lawyers are also well versed in procedure. They draft documents and interact with the court. They understand the local rules and how to do what is needed in your case. State procedures, obviously, can vary widely, but there can be significant distinctions even from county to county, and a good, experienced local attorney usually understands how to manage the idiosyncrasies of the local system. The details of those documents can also be crucial—miss a filing deadline, and you may give up your right to ever ask for alimony. These are the details that you pay a lawyer to manage for you, so that you can get on with the business of getting your life back on track.

Using an attorney can make a big difference in how you fare in your divorce. Your lack of knowledge or false assumptions about the law can hurt you, and hurt you big time. If you never talk to an attorney about your spouse's settlement proposal, or if you never have settlement papers reviewed by someone who can advocate for your interests, you could get the short end of the stick without even knowing it.

Even if you still trust your spouse, this is not a time to be foolhardy. You may be entitled to things you don't even know about. At the same time, your spouse may be consulting with an attorney without your knowing about it, so the playing field may not be as level as you believe. Don't assume, in other words, that your spouse's intentions are good just because your spouse tells you that his or her offer to you is fair and equitable. You can listen, as much or as little as you care to, to what your spouse has to say, but judge the offer yourself, based on all the information you need in order to evaluate the details. We strongly recommend that you have at least one meeting with an attorney to check out your understandings with an objective, trained person.

A lot of people put off going to see a lawyer. Delaying a visit with a lawyer is usually a major mistake. It is not hard, however, to understand the reasons so many people procrastinate in consulting with an attorney. Two of the most common reasons for not going to see an attorney are denial and a fear of being overwhelmed. Denial may have psychological roots ("My marriage isn't really all that bad—things are going to get better" or "Lawyers are scary, and I'd feel too intimidated" or "I can't talk to a stranger about all the distress I'm having or I'll fall apart"). Denial also may be linked to financial worries ("I can't afford the fees that lawyers charge" or "Even though I have the money and know I need a lawyer, the lawyer is going to bleed me dry and I don't know how to keep that from happening"). If you decide you need a lawyer, you should usually be able to find ways to surmount these psychological and financial barriers to getting legal representation for yourself.

Another reason that people don't go talk to attorneys is a lack of understanding about when and why lawyers should be consulted ("I don't need a lawyer right now" or "There's nothing a lawyer could do for me that I can't do for myself"). This reason for delay stems from a lack of familiarity with what lawyers do. Occasionally it stems from personal arrogance ("I'm sure I could do this better than someone else could"). Most people do realize, however, that lawyers have specialized knowledge and skills, but these same people may not recognize that divorce law is full of highly technical rules and traps for the unwary. The law is like poker, and maybe just as risky: if you don't know all the rules and how to play to win, you can lose the game.

People often don't realize that you don't need a lawyer only when you've been sued or have to go to court. Properly timed legal advice can help prevent certain problems from ever arising, and properly timed legal advice can potentially reduce the dimensions of existing problems. This kind of preventive use of a lawyer can save you heartache, time, and money. If you decide you need an attorney, go see one now, as soon as possible, rather than putting off the appointment.

# Finding a Lawyer You Will Like

People sometimes delay speaking with an attorney because they don't know how to go about finding the "right" lawyer for their particular problem. Consumers of professional and other services can be confused by too few or too many choices. Yet you've dealt with such questions in other parts of your life over and over again. Consider how frequently you face such questions: Have I picked the right babysitter for my children? Is this the right dentist or doctor for me to see? Which grocery store would be best for my family? Should I send my children to this public school?

Then consider how you've made these choices about the services that will best suit your needs. Sometimes you've applied common sense and economies of time and money to your choice ("I'd rather drive to the store two miles from my home than to a very similar store twenty miles away"). Sometimes you've relied on a personal referral because it leads you to exactly what you were looking for ("This is the only dentist in town who seems to be able to calm down frightened patients"). Sometimes you've picked a business or a professional based on general reputation ("They'll give you better repair service on your new Toyota than any other dealer in a two-hundred-mile radius" or "They get so many calls from all over the state that they know more about IBM computers than any other store around here").

The selection of an attorney who feels right to you is not so different from all these other kinds of choices that you make all the time regarding goods and services. You first think about what your priorities for legal services are. Then you decide how to gather information about the lawyers who would be available to you, so that you can see how certain lawyers mesh with your personal priorities. Finally, you make a choice based on criteria such as the amount of time and money you can put into finding the particular lawyer who will do the best job for you, the professional's reputation for specialized skills, the general reputation of the lawyer's firm within the community, and whether you sense this is a person whom you can trust.

Gathering the information you need is not as difficult as you might think. One easy way to gather information about attorneys is to ask people you trust and respect for leads, including not only the names of lawyer but also referrals to other people who might be able to suggest names. Friends, relatives, neighbors, casual acquaintances, and work associates are possible sources of leads, as are people you do business with. In particular, mental health professionals and clergy members who engage in crisis couples' counseling and general marriage counseling will probably have considerable information to share with you about the local domestic relations bar. You should also try to find out some of the names of a lawyer's satisfied clients (although you probably won't be able to obtain this information from the attorney directly, for the reason that a client or former client's name remains confidential unless the client consents to the disclosure). Then talk to clients or former clients about their personal experiences with the lawyer. People in your area who have actually been through separation and divorce can be your most valuable resources in selecting an attorney, as they will have formed opinions about their own lawyers and opposing counsel. You might also talk to other lawyers you know about a particular family law attorney's reputation.

Many state bar organizations maintain a referral list of attorneys willing to consult in specific subject areas for a minimum consultation fee. Meeting with a lawyer on this list may or may not help you locate a lawyer who has the appropriate experience and depth to manage your case. In some states, there may even be a statewide organization that represents those lawyers who are interested enough in domestic relations law to maintain membership in the family law subgroup of the state bar association. You should be able to obtain a list of the current members of such a group from the bar association headquarters in your state. Most state bar associations also sponsor some special programs you can inquire about, including, perhaps, a pro bono (no charge) volunteer lawyers program (VLP). Attorneys who have signed up for a VLP will sometimes take on family law cases at no charge. However, these programs generally have only minimal resources, and you cannot count on getting help from a VLP, which may receive many more requests than it can handle.

Another source of information is the courthouse personnel who regularly interact with local attorneys. These first-hand observers of attorneys in action may be far more valuable to your decision-making process than lawyer advertisements or the listings in various directories. Still, advertisements and directory entries can provide additional information about the kinds of cases a lawyer handles, where he or she went to school, and the colleagues with whom the lawyer practices. You might also ask, when you start visiting lawyers' offices, if the firm has a brochure that you can have.

The specialized training and knowledge of a lawyer you are considering is also something to inquire about. A lawyer who stays current with changes in the laws of property distribution, custody, child support, and alimony will most probably give you more expert advice. Similarly, a specialized lawyer's advice can be more custom tailored to your needs and goals because a specialist's depth will provide him or her with more creative and flexible solutions to new problems. As you do when you decide between a general medical practitioner and a specialist, you need to diagnose the complexity of the issues in your case before settling on the lawyer who could most properly advise you.

In North Carolina, the state bar permits attorneys to become certified in family law by passing a written examination and producing other proof of ability in the field. Lawyers who have become board certified in family law have demonstrated their overall experience and grasp of matrimonial and divorce issues. These practitioners sometimes charge higher rates, but you may actually save money by choosing a specialist. You may find that a board-certified lawyer can do the work at a faster pace and with less new research than generalists who know far less about the subtleties of matrimonial and divorce law. A list of board-certified attorneys is maintained by the bar and will be given out on request.

Most vital, of course, is that you meet any attorney who has been recommended to you before you decide if that lawyer is right for you. Your first contact with the lawyer may be by telephone. Sometimes the phone conversation alone tells you enough about the person to let you know whether you want to move on to the next step and actually schedule an office appointment. If you do decide to attend an initial meeting, plan to conduct your own interview of the lawyer to learn whether you feel your needs will be understood and adequately addressed by this particular lawyer.

This point cannot be made strongly enough. No matter how strongly a particular lawyer has been recommended to you, selecting an attorney is a highly personal matter. No one else should make this decision for you. This is, after all, the person you are possibly going to retain to safeguard your rights during a time of great emotional upheaval for you, to structure a settlement that is as favorable as possible to you, and to advise you on such highly technical matters as the potential tax consequences of a proposed settlement. Your sense of who the lawyer is as a person will be extremely important in predicting how much, and what kind of, attention the lawyer will give to your case. Because the lawyer with whom you consult, and whom you might decide to retain, can profoundly affect the course of your life and your children's lives, you want to make your selection very carefully.

Here are some signals you should watch for in the first meeting. If the lawyer you meet with does not strike you as a person in whom you can rest your confidence, as a person who will zealously act in your best interests, or as a person who can reach a resolution of your case efficiently and sensitively, move on. If your meeting did not result in a feeling of personal rapport or if you felt the lawyer was not very attentive to your questions and concerns, move on. Don't engage the lawyer if he or she appears to be disorganized, or if you can't follow most of what you're being told, or if you suspect the lawyer doesn't know the field very well.

First impressions are often lasting impressions. If you are uncomfortable with a lawyer's practice philosophy or style during an initial meeting, it is not likely you will grow to like this person a great deal more as time goes on. In one sense, picking a lawyer is a matter of personal taste. You are probably not going to feel very good anyway as you go through separation and divorce, given the huge emotional and financial issues you may be dealing with. There is absolutely no reason, then, to make yourself feel even worse by selecting a lawyer you just simply don't like.

Pay attention as well to your responses to the information you pick up during an office interview regarding the lawyer's policies, including fees.

At the outset you should be given a clear explanation of the attorney's billing and collection policies. Will you be billed at an hourly rate? If so, what is that rate? Does the rate vary among personnel in the firm? Are there different hourly rates for office and courtroom work? How will you be charged for other expenses, such as photocopying, secretarial time, postage, and like items? Are you expected to pay in advance of receiving services? If there is a "retainer" (initial advance deposit), is it refundable or nonrefundable if the work is terminated or completed before the entire deposit has been used? Is a flat fee (a fixed price for a defined legal job) available from this practice? Will your billing statements be sufficiently detailed for you to determine what exact work has been performed? Will there be a written fee agreement between you and your attorney?

Especially in domestic relations law, where the issues are so emotionally charged and clients are understandably under very great stress, the issue of fees can poison the relationship between client and lawyer if misunderstandings aren't cleared up early on. You are entitled to know how you will be charged for the work done for you, what other fees might be assessed to your case, and how you are expected to pay your bill. Don't settle for vague answers to questions about fees. No lawyer is likely to know exactly how much it will cost to handle your case; but every lawyer should be willing to tell you as much as he or she can about fees.

If the fee quoted to you is so low that it is almost too good to be true, that may be a very bad sign. Low fees usually mean one of two things: either the attorney is hungry for business (which may mean the lawyer is green behind the ears or that other people have found out this lawyer is not very good) or he or she doesn't really expect to finish your case for the quoted fee (which means the retainer amount is no indication of how much you will eventually spend). Do some sleuthing to determine if the attorney is a novice or if the quoted fee is unrealistic in light of the work that will need to be done.

If the quoted fee is unrealistic, that can also be a sign that the lawyer has lots of clients signing up at those bargain-basement prices. In a high-volume practice such as this, sometimes all those clients are poorly served because the lawyer has too little time to spend on each individual's case. Waits (for appointments, for returned phone calls, for work to be drafted, for court dates) can be long in such offices, and you may find that you have just gotten lost in the crowd. You may also wind up paying the "cheaper" lawyer more money in the long run, due to such a lawyer's lack of specialized knowledge and inefficiencies in the lawyer's office. In sum, large caseloads do not translate into quality legal services. Stay away from the lawyer who appears to offer large discounts.

It may be a good idea to have a mental or written checklist of questions to ask an attorney at your first meeting. Have along paper and pencil with which to take notes. You can add to the following list other special questions that apply to your own circumstances.

1. Who will work on my case?
2. What is the educational training and experience of the lawyers who will be working on my case? Have any of these lawyers published books or articles? What have they published? Do you have a copy that I can read?
3. How many cases like mine has your firm handled in the past year?
4. What are your average fees in cases such as mine? What do you think my case is going to cost?
5. How do you set your fees? What does the fee include?
6. What are your policies with regard to payment of fees, returning phone calls, providing copies of all correspondence and other documents, and keeping me informed about the progress of my case?
7. How long will I wait to get an appointment when I need to come in again? What hours are you available on the telephone and in the office?
8. Are my goals realistic? What problems can you foresee? How will we solve those problems?
9. How will you accomplish my goals? How long will it all take?
10. How often do you go to court? Do you prefer litigating a case or settling a case?

Based on the answers to your questions, your observations about the lawyer's style, and how you feel after the interview is over, you should be able to tell if the lawyer you've met with is right for you. Although initial interviews can be very intense, you should also experience some relief if you've met with a lawyer who will be good for you. If you notice that you are not feeling better after the meeting, that could be a signal to continue your search. When you find the right mix of energy, dedication, wisdom, and insight, you will recognize that is the lawyer for you.

## Understanding Attorney Fees

Would you like the inside scoop on how to get the best bargain on attorney fees? Here's the deal: it doesn't really matter how the fees are structured. What matters is that you pay attention to how much you're being charged. It may be a month before you get your first bill, and during that time, you could inadvertently spend far more than you can afford. It is perfectly reasonable for you to request a weekly itemization of time spent on your case, especially until that first bill comes. After a few weeks of careful analysis, you'll start to understand the pattern of charges, and you'll get a good sense of how *you* can control how much you ultimately spend on this divorce.

You will also preserve more property for yourself, of course, if part of your divorce planning takes minimizing your legal fees into account. But holding legal fees down should not be carried out in such a way that you become penny-wise and pound-foolish. Don't, for example, rely on your spouse's lawyer to do all the work. Opposing counsel is not safeguarding your interests, of that you can be certain. You *can* lower your own legal fees however, if your lawyer charges on an hourly basis, by avoiding long-winded telephone conversations and unnecessarily long meetings with your attorney; you can accomplish this by doing lots of the document "homework" on your own, by taking as reasonable a position as possible in negotiations, and by steering clear of protracted litigation. Document "homework," which is described at length in our chapter "Divorce and Finances," is an integral requirement for proper divorce planning. Read that chapter now, and then read it again later.

## Unbundled Legal Help

These are all important questions. But you don't have to engage an attorney full time to get the reassurance that can come from an affiliation with an attorney suited to your personal needs. Provided your marriage was relatively short, you have no children, and property issues are uncomplicated, having one or two meetings with a lawyer who understands your concerns and who can suggest ways for you to attain your goals might give you the tools you need to represent yourself. Those tools can empower you despite all the turmoil people experience during the early stages of separation. Even if you were married for years and accumulated considerable property, but you intend to manage many details of your separation without the constant oversight of an attorney, having a sympathetic and sensitive lawyer with whom you can periodically consult can provide peace of mind in a way nothing else can.

A top-notch lawyer may be beyond your means, but that is no excuse for "going it all by yourself" if you don't absolutely have to. If you choose an attorney wisely, using the techniques recommended in this chapter, you should be able to navigate the treacherous emotional waters of separation and divorce with far less difficulty. Your mental and emotional state will be less disrupted by the process of divorce if you can associate with an attorney who has a solid understanding of both the law and human nature. On the flip side, if you pick the wrong lawyer, your life could become sheer hell. A difficult, disruptive, unpleasant lawyer can turn an amicable situation into a protracted litigation matter that drags on for years.

## Getting the Most from Meeting a Lawyer

When you go for your initial consultation with a lawyer, there are several things you can do to ensure you get as much information as possible from that first meeting. If the website (or the initial phone call) suggests materials or documents that you can bring to that first meeting, follow those instructions carefully. You don't want to waste your time or money by showing up unprepared.

Try to think through your questions about how this divorce process is going to look ahead of time. It may be hard to organize your thoughts at this early stage; try writing down as much as possible. If you go in with a written list of questions, you're less likely to forget to ask something important. By the same token, take careful notes during the meeting. You may even want to consider bringing along a support person to help you keep track of the details. Finally, if you leave the office with a packet of information, a book, forms to fill out, or anything else that will help streamline the process, do your homework thoroughly and carefully.

## Helping Your Lawyer Help You

As divorce lawyers with years of experience, we have a few suggestions for you, as the client, to help you get the best representation possible.

1. Please be polite. We're here to help you; we are not the enemy. While divorce can be an emotionally charged process, try to remember that your attorney really is on your side.

2. Please ask questions. We can't know exactly how much you understand about what's happening unless you let us know when something doesn't make sense.

3. By the same token, please try to understand the explanations we give you; if we have to answer the same question over and over, we can't move on to the next issue that needs to be dealt with.

4. If we ask you to do some "homework," please be as thorough and accurate as possible. The court system often requires very specific documentation, and often you are the only person who can provide those materials.

5. Please be prompt, both to appointments and to court. Likewise, please take appointments seriously—we can't help you if you don't show up.

6. 6. Finally, please be truthful. If you are not forthcoming with the details of your situation or your life, we can't anticipate how best to handle your case. The attorney-client relationship implies, and requires, a certain level of trust. We recognize that trusting a near stranger with the most intimate details of your life, at a time when that life seems to be disintegrating, can be a real leap of faith, but it can also be the first step toward getting that life back on track.

# Domestic Violence

At this juncture, we need to point out that in situations where one spouse is abusive, much of the usual divorce "wisdom" may not apply. Domestic violence, by definition, occurs in relationships in which there is a significant imbalance of power. Under those circumstances, mediation or collaboration clearly won't work—any system that requires parties to negotiate from positions of equality will automatically favor a spouse who has some measure of control over the other, even if that control is very subtle, or even unrecognized by the abused party.

---

## Separation Violence

The first major step in any divorce process is separation; if you are in an abusive marriage, that first step will look different for you than it will for someone in a more peaceful situation. When a woman leaves her batterer, her risk of serious violence or death increases dramatically; it's crucial to keep this in mind and proceed with caution. Statistics paint a grim picture: [11]

- Separated/divorced women are fourteen times more likely than married women to report having been a victim of violence by their spouse or ex-spouse.
- Women separated from their husbands were three times more likely to be victimized by spouses than divorced women, and twenty-five times more likely to be victimized by spouses than married women.
- 65 percent of intimate homicide victims physically separated from the perpetrator prior to their death.

A woman who makes the decision to leave an abusive spouse needs to be mindful, always, that safety is her first priority. The first step should be to make a safety plan. You may need to spend some time gathering the necessary components of your safety plan, but of course, if you feel that you are in imminent danger, you may have no choice but to leave on a moment's notice with nothing but the clothes you are wearing.

If you have the luxury of planning your departure and leaving when it suits you, consider the following points:

Try to gather some money, or even credit, that you can get your hands on quickly and easily. Abusers often control their partners by denying them access to the family cash and accounts, and a complete lack of financial resources can prohibit a battered spouse from leaving at a crucial moment. It's essential to be able to walk out the door at any moment and know that you can scrape together the basics of survival for yourself—and perhaps your children—for at least a few days, until you can get some help.

Important documents: Once you leave an abusive home, you may not be able to safely go back. If there are documents that may be important to proving your case or your financial situation, you should try to assemble those items prior to your departure. Again, safety is always the highest priority—don't do anything to make the situation worse than it already is—but a file folder of things like photocopied credit card bills, income tax forms, and bank statements can make your situation much easier to sort through when you do finally get to sit down with an attorney. Hang onto your health insurance card; be sure to include your passport and/or driver's license in that folder. It might be much easier to gather things in one place before you need them than it will be to go back and replace them later.

Contact information: if there is even a remote chance that you could suddenly find yourself out on the street with nowhere to go, you should make a list of numbers you can call in an emergency. Start with the obvious: 9-1-1. If at any point your safety is at risk, call the police. It's a good idea to also know how to contact your local domestic violence shelter. Many communities have a safe house, where an abuse victim can stay, in hiding, long enough to get her act together and make longer-term arrangements that will enable her to move on with her life while staying safe. Finally, you'll want to keep with you the phone numbers of a friend or relative or two who could help you out in an emergency.

---

# The Divorce Process in Abusive Marriages

It's important to remember, throughout the process of separation and divorce, that much of the advice that is normally given to divorcing couples may not apply in a domestic violence situation. Normal conflict resolution behaviors may not be possible, and the alternatives may seem counterintuitive. While a "normal" divorce process may require and reward negotiation strategies, it may be necessary for a battered spouse to forego the compromises that can lead to amicable resolution for many couples. A controlling spouse will often hijack the negotiation process to perpetuate the cycle of abuse. We often see an abuser engage in stall tactics to prolong control; sometimes the only alternative is to go to court. An attorney sensitive to some of the psychological issues surrounding domestic violence can be instrumental in helping the survivor discern when the "normal" process isn't working, and when more drastic measures are warranted.

As much as we believe in and recommend the mediation process as a means of reducing conflict during the termination of a marriage, we recognize that it is often not appropriate for situations in which domestic violence is occurring. Mediation theory dictates that participating parties need to be equals in terms of the balance of power in the relationship. Any situation in which one partner has a measure of control over the other will not lend itself to a calm, rational negotiation process. In domestic violence cases, we have found that it is often necessary to let the case go to court—which we usually don't like to do in nonviolent situations—so that a judge can intervene, hopefully breaking the cycle of violence by ensuring that *both* parties are heard and represented.

The presence of children in an abusive marriage can complicate the divorce dramatically. Much of the advice is the same—battles over custody issues can become yet another tool the abuser uses to control his victim—but when a parent is concerned about the safety of her/his children, the stakes often *seem* much higher. There are certain systemic biases that can make custody negotiations even more difficult for an abused spouse. For instance, the court system generally exhibits what is called the "friendly parent bias"—the flexible, agreeable parent gets more sympathy from the court, but flexibility is rarely an option for a victim of domestic violence.

Let's consider the case of "Jane." Her priority must always be safety, for herself and for her children. She may find herself within a framework of restraining orders, supervised visitation, public meeting places, and carefully scheduled exchanges that leave little room for flexibility but that she relies on to ensure her own safety. Another concern many abused mothers express is that, because she shares children with her abuser, she will never be able to truly pull up stakes and move away for the abuser altogether. There is no easy answer in these situations; we just go back to our most important piece of advice: safety comes first.

If violence in your home escalates to the point that you feel that you are in danger, immediate action is warranted, and even required. You will need to:

- Call the police and get a police report
- Get a protective order
- File criminal assault charges
- Find safe shelter

The website of the American Bar Association is an excellent resource to consult if you find you have to flee a violent situation.

One important thing to remember when it comes to involving the police in a domestic dispute is that it only works if the abuser respects authority. Someone who has been in trouble a lot is unlikely to abide by an order. Experts say the survivor is the best judge of what will keep him/her safe. A police officer won't be able to protect you around the clock, and a domestic violence order is not a bulletproof vest. You know that if the police can't protect the president from getting shot, they can't stop a violent spouse. Survivors have to take matters into their own hands and go to a shelter or hotel to hide. If you find you absolutely do not have the money to get to a safe place, think outside the box a little.

You might be surprised to find that there are people in your life who are concerned about your welfare and are more than willing to help. Even employers and churches have been known to pay for a hotel room for a few days to enable an abuse victim to hide out and pick him or herself back up.

When it comes to actually involving law enforcement and pressing charges against an abuser, there are a couple of things to remember. Every state, of course, is different, but in general, a restraining order is a civil document requiring one party to stay away from another. Such an order usually outlines very clear boundaries, or parameters: the defendant can't come within a certain number of feet of the plaintiff, or only in certain public places, or with very specific supervision/protection in place. These orders are generally passed in family court. But if, on the other hand, you file criminal charges, the case will be heard in criminal court, and will carry the potential of jail time if the offender is found guilty. A list of charges that are generally considered domestic violence crimes in most states would include the following:

- Assault, or assault on a female
- Making harassing phone calls
- Stalking
- Interference with a 9-1-1 call
- Strangulation

Again, as we have pointed out, laws governing domestic violence vary widely from state to state. Efforts have been made to standardize legislation across the country, but if you have questions regarding the law where you live, you'll need to consult a local attorney.

Finally, before we leave the topic of domestic violence, we would like to give several pieces of advice, accumulated over our combined years of experience working directly for abused spouses, but also working to improve the legal code that is meant to protect victims of domestic violence. First, trust your instincts. If your gut tells you that you're in danger, get to a safe place. Second, don't let other people in your life minimize your situation. Only you know what you're going through, and your own experience has to inform your decisions. And finally, don't assume that anyone else's stories apply to you. Every situation is unique, and relying on rumor and gossip to guide your actions can be a recipe for disaster. Get professional help, and stay safe.

# Notes

[11] Bernice R. Kennedy, PhD., *Domestic Violence A.K.A. Intimate Partner Violence (IPV)* (Lincoln: iUniverse, 2007).

# Life During Divorce

Most of our clients have a lot of questions about how to handle the period between the time they decide to divorce and the end of the process. This can be a challenging time, especially if you or your spouse are dealing with the intense emotions that usually arise after one of you makes the decision to end the marriage. There are many legal and practical minefields to avoid. In this chapter we will answer most of the questions you are likely to have about living through this period including:

- How can my spouse and I share parenting if we cannot talk without fighting?
- How can I get through the separation if I have no money to support myself or my children?
- Is it all right if I date during my separation?
- What if my spouse and I have sex while separated?
- Can I do anything during separation to improve my chances of success in court?

Many couples stay separated for more than a year, due to either legal requirements or choice. That is too long to live in limbo. During this time you will want to be transitioning into your post-divorce life, but you need to be careful to do what is necessary to achieve the goals you set for your divorce.

## Building a New Relationship with Your Spouse

Once it becomes clear that you and your spouse will divorce, you begin a new phase of your relationship. If you have minor children, this new relationship will be a long-lasting one in which you will need to work together to parent your kids. If no children are involved, you and your spouse will need a relationship that at least allows you to work together to resolve the issues of your divorce without getting into an expensive courtroom fight. The keys to building this new relationship are sensitivity and open communication.

We discussed earlier the emotions that people often feel as they go through the divorce transition. It is most often the case that you and your spouse will be at different stages in grieving over the loss of the relationship. One of you may have already begun to build a new identity as a single person while the other may still be dealing with anger, depression, or guilt.

During the divorce, you will both need to be sensitive and aware of the stage you and your spouse are at in the transition. If your spouse is still dealing with the intense emotions usually experienced in the early stages of divorce, it will be best for you both if you proceed slowly, even if you are feeling anxious to move on. Pushing a person in this state, or being pushed when you are feeling vulnerable, is likely to result in defensive action that is likely to work against both of your long-term goals.

Being aware of your spouse's emotional state is different from trying to improve his or her state of mind. While you have likely depended on each other for emotional support during the marriage, it is no longer your responsibility to satisfy your spouse's emotional needs. Of course, if both of you choose to, you're perfectly welcome to continue such interdependency. However, doing so could delay the process of personal growth for one or both of you and might create a burden on one of you. It is probably better for you both if you work to develop independence and other sources of support.

Unlike in your courtship, when emotion likely ruled the day, a successful divorce, along with a successful post-divorce relationship, requires the triumph of logic over emotion. You will want to evaluate each of your actions during the divorce process to consider whether what you are about to do furthers your goals for your divorce or is a purely emotional action or response that gets you nowhere, or even makes things worse.

The types of actions that can be highly destructive to the comity required for negotiations include limiting access to shared assets. We wrote earlier about protecting yourself financially during separation. There are many reasonable steps that should be taken such as closing or freezing joint credit and checking accounts. However, even if you may intend it purely as a protective measure, an unannounced removal of access to assets will almost inevitably lead your spouse to conclude that the action was taken with the intent to cause hurt. Your now-wounded ex is then are likely to react to this perceived attack in a way that might complicate your situation. The bottom line is that you should take protective actions, but you should communicate with your spouse as much as possible to avoid him or her finding out that the credit card is no longer good at the checkout counter.

If communications between you and your spouse broke down as your marriage came to an end, you will want to work to reopen dialogue. This may mean that you simply need to listen without fighting back as your spouse vents anger at the situation. Your goal should be to get past this stage so you can reestablish rapport. Doing so can save you both a great deal in the divorce process. Some couples find that once they move out of the roles of husband and wife, they are able to enjoy a better relationship than they had during the marriage.

---

# Parenting while Separated

Divorce creates significant new challenges for you as a parent. In many divorces, our legal system unhelpfully pushes parents into adversarial roles at a time when they need to work together to parent their children. We provide a great deal of information about how to best arrange for the long-term care of your children in our chapters on child custody and child support later in the book. Here we will focus on the things you need to consider as you begin the divorce process. Most of the behaviors we encourage you to adopt will also be important to continue even after the divorce is final. Ultimately, as we have said before, if you can step back from some of the tangled emotions of the divorce itself and make decisions as neutrally as possible, you will find that you are a better parent— and a healthier person—in the long run.

During the divorce process, you will need to speak regularly to your spouse about your children. If you have agreed to share custody you will need to, at a minimum, arrange for pickups/drop-offs and exceptions. It is important that both of you regard these conversations more as business meetings than opportunities to rehash the problems that led to your divorce. Parenting conversations are not the time to blame your spouse for what has happened. Do your best to take responsibility for your own feelings. The same rules apply when delivering or collecting your children. This time is likely to be awkward for everyone. Don't make it worse by discussing touchy issues or rebuking your spouse if he or she is late, if the kids are a mess, or if they haven't eaten the way you think they should. You can address these types of issues at a later time without involving the kids.

As you begin to co-parent during your divorce there are a number of issues you will need to work through. Expect to make some mistakes as you learn the ropes, and be careful not to expect your spouse to be perfect right off the bat.

One mistake too many parents make is criticizing their spouse in front of the children. It may seem obvious that this is a bad idea, but divorcing parents, often feeling intense betrayal and hurt, can denigrate their spouse in subtle ways without even realizing it. For example, a parent is late for visitation exchange and the other parent mumbles, "Typical behavior." A child wonders, "Typical of what?" You have for years trained your child to hear and respond to the tone of your voice. So, yes, they hear the tone. Don't fool yourself. Remember, your child is a product of both of you. When you criticize the other parent, you are potentially criticizing part of the child. This is, of course, something no parent would intentionally try to do. You want your child to have the confidence and self-esteem to enter adulthood successfully. Choices you make now, even in the heat of the moment, can influence your child's success later. Take a deep breath and wait to make the comment until your child is safely out of range.

Parents going through a divorce often put their children in the middle in inappropriate ways, even sometimes using them as go-betweens and spies. Both of these actions only lead to problems. Your children do not need the extra burden of being responsible for communicating your expectations about bed time or drop off to your spouse. They also do not need to be put in the awkward position of possibly betraying one parent when being pumped for information by the other. You not only want to avoid using your children as your mouthpiece or spy, but you also need to avoid encouraging them to keep secrets from your spouse. This behavior puts kids in the difficult position of having to lie to or betray one or both parents.

Some parents use their children as pawns during divorce. They feel that by denying access to the children they will somehow be able to get even with a spouse. Unless there is abuse involved, cutting off or excessively limiting your spouse's access to the children is likely to work against you. It is very rare that a parent will not be given access to children if the matter is taken to court, and your cutting off access now could lead your spouse to escalate things legally. This may introduce a judge into the equation, which can greatly decrease your degree of control over what happens to your children.

All parents fear that they will lose their children through the divorce. Sometimes parents fight for months over the term "joint custody," mainly out of this fear of loss. You are not responsible for the feelings of your spouse, but remember that life will be much easier for you if your spouse is not fighting you at every turn in your child's life. Make the way easier for yourself. Tell your spouse everything and anything about the children. If you are at the stage when you can't bear the thought of talking to your spouse again, use carefully worded e-mails. If you think your spouse doesn't care or doesn't want to know, do it anyway. At a minimum you get extra credit points later if you have to go to court. And your child might find out that his/her parents are proud enough of his/her achievements to talk about them.

Most parents are surprised when their children resist going to the other parent's household. But it happens, especially in the beginning and often even under the best of circumstances. Why does it happen? Good question. Maybe your child is expressing some of the anxiety and discomfort that everyone in the family is feeling about the changes. Maybe your child wants to continue playing on the Sony PlayStation and doesn't like the interruption. Either way, it would behoove both you and your spouse to help your child as much as possible during this time. Talk with your child and problem solve together. Is he getting hungry? Does he hate the drive? Encourage your child and remind him or her of the enjoyable things he or she will get to do. Repress your own anxiety and resentment about the custodial situation. This new life is your child's life now. Remind yourself that regardless of the circumstances, you do want your child to be happy in this new life.

When you were married and living together, you knew that your children got different things from each parent. Maybe one parent was better at nurturing while another was better at encouraging the kids to take risks. Maybe one parent handled the math homework better than the spelling. Either way, remember that your child can still benefit from these differences. There was something that attracted you to your spouse long ago. Remember that somewhere, deep down, those positive qualities might still exist in your spouse, and your child can learn from them to hopefully grow into a loving, confident adult.

Finally, parents in divorce need to be careful to not rely on their children for emotional support. Many kids are eager to do whatever they can to help a parent going through a period of depression. They can also be easy allies when adults are venting anger. Children are dealing with many adjustments during the divorce process. You and your spouse need to avoid putting additional burdens on them. Even though children may appear quite mature, it is rarely appropriate or helpful for them to become an adult's support system. Children in divorce need to be on the receiving end of emotional support from you, not the other way around.

---

# Temporary Orders

Due to state laws and the time required to emotionally prepare for finalizing negotiations, the period between the decision to divorce and the completion of the legal process is often lengthy. We previously advised you to try to negotiate, before you separate, an agreement that defines how finances will be handled during this period. We also advised you to carefully protect your assets so that you can have access to them without causing a legal flare up. Of course, many people find themselves separated without an agreement and with their assets inaccessible. These are the kinds of situations where temporary court orders can help.

If you are dependent on your spouse financially or will have custody of the children and have not arranged for at least interim support, you can ask the court for temporary orders for support and custody. A temporary order is usually granted within a few days and will remain in effect until either you settle or you have a full court hearing. If the party seeking the temporary order is the same party who files the divorce petition, then both matters should be filed at the same time. If the party seeking the temporary order did not file the petition, then that spouse should file the request for the temporary order as soon as possible.

While we emphasize the importance of reaching settlements without involving the court, temporary orders can be an exception. If one or both of you are unwilling to quickly create a temporary solution for finances and custody, waiting to act can be detrimental, especially if you are financially dependent or responsible for the care of your children. If you become financially distressed, you might be willing to agree to an unreasonable settlement in order to regain stability. Thinking longer term, when it comes to property division, if one spouse has sole access to community property, it can become easier for that person to create the appearance that the assets are separate property.

Temporary orders may also be your only route if you experience problems or concerns with the handling of child custody. If you are having trouble getting your children back during visits or have reason to believe your spouse is going to attempt to disappear with the children, a temporary order may help make your expectations clear. Of course, a court order cannot truly stop someone from taking an action, but it can increase the consequences of that action.

# Dating During Divorce

Some people going through a divorce cannot imagine reentering the dating scene. Others begin dating to distract themselves from the emotional pain of divorce, or to help deal with the loneliness they feel without their spouse. During this period you are going through many emotional changes. Your ideas about what you want or need from a relationship are likely to be continually in flux as you reestablish your independence. The statistics show that relationships begun during or shortly after divorce have only a slim chance of lasting very long.

Although many people ignore the advice, every professional that deals with people going through divorce recommends avoiding getting into new relationships at least until your divorce is final, and usually for a year after that. If you began an adulterous relationship prior to discussing the divorce with your spouse, it is best to put the relationship on hold until the divorce is final. If the relationship was meant to be, it will survive the hiatus. Relationships of this nature that are revealed during the divorce could result in your spouse adding fault grounds to your divorce filing—in states where that is possible—regardless of whether the claim is valid. If you are considering revealing the relationship because you feel guilty, be sure to understand how your actions might affect your property distribution or alimony. You might feel better about yourself but later regret the financial implications.

Aside from the potential for additional emotional upheaval and complication, dating during divorce can work against your efforts to resolve the issues involved in your divorce quickly and inexpensively. You may have reached an emotional disconnection from your spouse, but he or she might still be emotionally attached to you. Even if your spouse appears to be accepting the divorce, he or she can become jealous and angry when faced with the fact that you are dating, or living with, someone else. Obviously such emotions work against any efforts at an amicable and rapid resolution of the issues in your divorce.

Couples with children need to be particularly aware of how their actions will affect their kids. A parent who dates during divorce is likely to alienate the children. The kids are more likely to blame a parent who rapidly moves into a new relationship for ruining the marriage. They also are likely to demonize your new companion. If the opposite happens and they begin to build a relationship with the new person, you may be setting them up for another blow, given the odds of such a rebound relationship succeeding. If your children have to experience yet another loss, the potentially harmful effects of the divorce on them can be amplified.

Dating during divorce carries with it risks of complicating your negotiations and harming your children's emotional health. Dating, and especially living together, can also affect you financially, either in negotiations or in court. A spouse seeking support from a soon-to-be ex may find it more difficult to justify financial needs, particularly when living with a new person. On the other hand, a spouse who might have to pay alimony can find that moving in with someone and thus lowering household expenses may result in the ex-spouse or a judge deciding that the support payment should be increased. Although child support is more formulaic than spousal support, judges can deviate from the state guidelines. A case where living expenses are affected by the sharing of expenses with a new companion could trigger such a deviation. Even if, like most, you do not end up in court, the effect on your finances of your living arrangement could play a part in your efforts to negotiate a settlement.

The final area of concern regarding dating during divorce is potentially the most significant. If you are forced to go to court to work out a child custody arrangement, your fitness as a parent will be evaluated by a judge, and possibly an expert assisting the court, who will have very little information about you. If your children are, as often happens, uncomfortable being around you while you are with your new companion, your relationship with them may be, at least temporarily, damaged at a time when that relationship is being scrutinized. You should also realize that someone evaluating your parenting might view your decision to date during divorce as evidence of a lack of regard for the feelings of your children. Such a conclusion could affect the amount of parenting time you are awarded. Moving in with someone during your divorce greatly increases the potential negative impact on your case.

If, despite all the potential consequences, you choose to date during your divorce, do so discreet to avoid harming your negotiations and, most importantly, hurting your children. Definitely wait until a relationship seems well established before involving your children with your new companion.

# Sex with Spouse

Another issue that comes up during divorce is whether it is all right to have sex with the person you are divorcing. To many this will seem like a highly unlikely possibility. However, couples in the process of divorcing sometimes seek comfort from each other and revert to old patterns.

There are several problems that can arise when a couple resumes sexual relations during the divorce process. First, if you are involved in a fault-based divorce, you could jeopardize your fault claim if you consent to being with your spouse after the claim is made. Second, you obviously increase the emotional complexity of your situation when you renew your sexual relationship. One or the other may still see the possibility for reconciliation. It is unlikely that both of you will have the same feelings about the meaning of the sex. Resulting misunderstandings can lead to a flare up that makes your divorce harder. Finally, if children are involved and they find a parent returning to the house for a night, you will fuel their very real hopes and fantasies that their parents will reunite. This is unfair and emotionally damaging.

# Creating and Maintaining Distance

The process of transitioning from being one half of a couple to being independent again can be difficult. During the divorce process, you will want to begin to create and maintain emotional distance between yourself and your spouse. This does not mean that you need be impolite. On the contrary, you are best served by being as polite as you can be. Part of being polite is having respect for each other's privacy. This can be a challenge if you are dealing with jealousy or have an irrepressible curiosity about how your spouse is faring, whether there is a third party involved, or what your ex is thinking about you. Focusing on your spouse makes the process of returning to your independence more difficult. If you see yourself exerting much time and energy finding out about and reacting to your spouse's life, consider getting some help from a friend or counselor to so that you can focus on creating your own independent life. This is your chance to start your new life free of the problems that broke up your last marriage; staying enmeshed in that past will not help you move forward.

The jealousy or anger that can arise during the divorce process can be intense. It is obvious that feelings that turn into violent action constitute domestic violence. What is less obvious is that doing things such as calling your spouse after being told not to—or pursuing contact at home, work, or anywhere else after being told stay away—can be cause for legal action, including your former spouse filing for a harassment restraining order. If you are the victim of such harassment, we will explain your options in our chapter "Domestic Violence."

On the other hand, if you have thought about clever ways to "get back" at your spouse, you need to think again. Your actions may result in restriction of your rights by means of a restraining order, a significant reduction in the likelihood of successful negotiations with your spouse, and the creation of a hurdle to overcome when it comes to convincing a judge that you are a reasonable person. If you see yourself going down this road, get some help in managing your emotions right away. Anger is an important emotion that doesn't need to be denied, eliminated, or suppressed. However, it is critical that it be controlled to the point that it does not overtake rational thought and cause harmful behavior. If you don't get help on your own, you may soon find a judge forcing you to do so. Such a loss of control is something to be avoided if at all possible.

While some have trouble not prying into the former spouse's life, others have trouble creating a degree of privacy. A woman who has lived for years in a controlling relationship can have great trouble adjusting to the fact that she no longer needs to report to her spouse; she may be overly willing to share details related to the divorce. Some people may feel uncomfortable or guilty keeping secrets from the ex-spouse, or putting their own needs first. This is obviously a dangerous situation when it comes to negotiations. Although emotions and relationship history inevitably play some part in divorce, it is important to approach negotiations in a business-like manner. Be careful about what you share and when. Ideally, if you are the weaker spouse in a controlling relationship, you will engage a lawyer to represent you in your negotiations. This will allow you to politely direct your spouse to talk with your lawyer if he or she presses you for information or attempts to engage you in negotiations outside of meetings where your lawyer is present.

# Maintaining Appearances

Although most divorces are settled outside of court, the possibility that a judge will decide one or more of the issues in your divorce is almost always present. Because of this, you must consider your actions during the divorce in light of how they might affect you in court. People with knowledge of your personal life may become witnesses in court, especially if you are involved in a custody trial. It is to your great advantage to present yourself carefully in front of these potential witnesses.

One spouse may be having trouble keeping cool under the stress of divorce. To someone with a limited view of that person's parenting, he or she may seem impatient and easy to anger. The other spouse may be intentionally working overtime on appearing to be the perfect parent in order to gain advantage in the custody case. Someone witnessing the family over this period may certainly have a distorted view of events, but could be an effective witness for one side in court. It is unfortunate, but you need to remember that you may be "under the microscope" during the divorce process, so do what you can to create a positive impression of yourself.

Because the people with some knowledge of your personal life might be witnesses in court, you need to avoid creating enemies while the divorce is ongoing. Firing the nanny or housekeeper could create an enemy who is more than happy to speak out on behalf of your spouse. Rather

than engendering animosity, you will want to be cultivating positive relationships with those who interact with or simply observe your family.

# Part Two:
# The Major Divorce Decisions

# Property Division: Whose Stuff is it Anyway?

When you begin to think about separating from your spouse, you will need to consider very carefully how your property will be divided. During the course of your marriage, however short it might have been, the two of you have likely accumulated some amount of *stuff*: both the obvious, tangible stuff—such as a house, cars, a CD collection, china, pets, water-skis—and less visible property, such as savings accounts, life insurance policies, retirement plans, stock market investments, or business ownership. All of this *stuff* will need to be split up or shared; what was one household will have to become two. How well you weather that transition to your separate household may be a function of how carefully you think through and plan for the division of your marital property.

Each state has its own laws defining the concept of marital property, but generally speaking, things that were bought or accumulated during the marriage using funds earned during the marriage are considered marital property and will be divided. As we pointed out earlier, this can vary from state to state, so you may need to consult a local attorney to get more specific information regarding things like inheritances, gifts, or things/money that were acquired prior to the marriage. Regardless, when a marriage ends, you will need to think through all the assets and debts that you and your partner hold (remember that inventory you did several chapters ago?), and develop a strategy for splitting it all up.

The process used to divide property can vary pretty dramatically from case to case, but generally speaking, there are two basic elements: you can physically divide the *stuff* ("I'll take the couch, you get the chairs"), or you can agree on the monetary value of the items at issue, sell them, and split the proceeds. However, we need to reiterate: the earlier in your separation you and your spouse can reach an agreement, the less the entire divorce process will cost you, both financially and emotionally.

It will be enormously helpful—if you haven't already done so—for you to make an inventory of all of your marital property; your attorney should ask you to do so, if you don't bring such a list to your first meeting. Now, for some couples, that list is pretty short and simple, everyone is in agreement, and property distribution can be taken care of with a minimum of bickering. But in most cases, even if you are both fairly amicable, you will want an attorney to confirm that the division of assets is equitable. In truly bitter break-ups, a judge will need to make the final decision about how the property is to be distributed.

First off, if you own a home, you will need to divide it. This will most likely necessitate a real estate appraisal (one of those professional services we talked about in the chapter "Divorce and Finances"). Once you know what your home is worth, you have a choice: you can sell it, and divide the proceeds, or one of you can purchase the home from the other (this is sometimes a particularly attractive option if there are children involved who would benefit from the continuity of staying in familiar surroundings). Selling a home can take time; so don't expect this particular piece of your settlement to be wrapped up quickly. Be patient, and expect a certain amount of uncertainty in your life for a while.

Business ownership can complicate property division even more. In some marriages, one partner owns a business outright, or with partners outside the marriage, while the other spouse has nothing to do with the business. In other situations, a couple owns a business together. In either case, the wisest plan is to hire a business appraiser, and rely on that person's assessment of how the business should be valued and divided. Now, some couples are so embittered by the time they get to this stage in the process that they can't even manage to hire the appraiser without acrimony: it sometimes becomes necessary for each spouse to hire his or her own appraiser, then allow their attorneys to work together to reconcile the two valuations. Understand that you may walk away from such a situation feeling that you didn't get what you wanted, and that this feeling is normal—such is the nature of compromise. It's usually worth the compromise to be able to get the property divided so that you can move on with your life.

One question that we often hear is whether or not a professional license constitutes marital property. The answer, in most states, is, no. Most states do not divide the value of the degree. Generally speaking, even if you put your spouse through medical school, that medical degree itself cannot be divided. The resultant medical practice, of course, is a business, and will need to be valued and dealt with accordingly, as per the above paragraph.

Retirement plans are yet another asset that gets divided at the end of a marriage. For the most part, we are using the word *divided* loosely here: in the case of a retirement plan, what usually happens is *the cash value* of the plan goes on the marital balance sheet, and the assets are allocated in such a way that each party gets an equal portion. In other words, if the house is worth $100,000 and the 401k is worth the same amount, one of you might take the house, while the other gets the 401k.

Sometimes, however, retirement plans are literally divided. They're split in half. Most plans are subject to special taxation laws that complicate their division. The process of dividing these plans requires submitting a special document to the court for signature. This QDRO facilitates either (1) direct payments from the plan to the nonemployee spouse or (2) the creation of a separate retirement account for the nonemployee spouse. The QDRO is essential in order to avoid incurring taxes on the division of the plan.

Stock options are an important and valuable asset in many families. They are often worth a great deal of money. The division of the options may require cooperation from the employer as well as special documentation. Generally, however, these assets are divided in a manner similar to other investments.

Inheritances can complicate matters. If one spouse has received a significant inheritance, most states (not all) will treat that as separate property—*depending what was done with the money.* Some states have exceptions: in North Carolina, for instance, inherited money remains the property of the spouse who received it, unless it's used to purchase jointly titled real estate, at which point it becomes marital property. Of course, the paper trail becomes significant here: if you inherited $10,000 from Grandma, and you want to have that much added to your side of the ledger, you'll need to document that the money was spent in such a way that it doesn't get caught up in any of the potential exceptions. And again, those exceptions vary from state to state: check with your attorney.

And while we're on the subject of dividing property, we need to point out that marital debt (including unpaid taxes) will be divided just like marital assets. Some states will recognize an exception to that rule, for debt incurred that was not for the benefit of the marriage (services of a prostitute, for instance), but those exceptions are few and difficult to prove. Even if one spouse incurs significant debt without the knowledge of the other, that debt is generally considered marital property, and thus both parties are on the hook for it.

# Alimony: Only Part of the Solution

Another significant piece of the financial implications of a divorce is the question of alimony. Alimony consists of payments made toward the support of one spouse by the other. The concept is rooted in the historical notion that a wife was dependent on her husband, and he had an obligation to support her even if he chose to end the marriage. The more contemporary definition posits that alimony helps minimize the broader social/financial impact of divorce, by (theoretically) ensuring that large numbers of formerly dependent spouses are not suddenly relying on the state for the support that was once provided within the family structure. It is *not* designed to be punitive, nor is it meant to be a weapon used in the waging of the larger war that divorce so often becomes. As much as possible, both parties need to look at alimony as a purely financial, pragmatic question that needs to be answered as systematically and neutrally as possible.

The first question that has to be answered during alimony negotiations is that of financial need. In order for one spouse to be *required* to pay alimony, the recipient of those payments will need to prove that he or she will be subject to a drastically reduced standard of living when the marriage ends. In many states, this is the only relevant question. There are still a few vestiges, around the country, of the old system that held that *fault* also figured into the equation; in North Carolina, for instance, as of this writing, adultery on the part of the dependent spouse can render that person ineligible for alimony. But that behavioral link varies dramatically from state to state, so it's always best to check with a local attorney.

Another thing to remember is that, as with most of the issues surrounding a divorce, it is possible to reach an amicable agreement out of
court, but it is equally possible to fight and claw every step of the way,
ultimately relying on a judge to issue a court order, which can be much
harder to renegotiate down the road. It is almost always to the advantage
of all parties involved to settle the issues before they go to trial. Judges in
most states rely on a formula to determine the actual amount of monthly
alimony payments; it is not uncommon for that number to feel like a major hardship to the payer, but completely inadequate to the payee, simply
because they both gave up their vested interest in a compromise amount
when they took the case to court. It is crucial, *especially* when negotiations
become heated, to try and look beyond the raw emotion of the break-up
and focus on the long-term financial issues.

If you are the supporting spouse, your inclination may be to try and
whittle the payments down as much as possible; it is understandable that
you wouldn't want to feel that you are handing over a significant portion
of your paycheck to your ex. But if your ex was truly a dependent
spouse—perhaps a stay-at-home parent?—then you need to consider the
bigger picture of how reduced circumstances will affect your children.
You may not want to give one red cent to your ex, but do you want your
children to have to move out of the house they've always lived in? Will
the dependent parent of your toddler have to go back to work full-time,
putting the child in daycare, if you balk at the idea of alimony? It can be
tough to separate the financial issues from the emotional, but particularly
if there are children involved, you need to rise above your instincts and
consider the long-term structure of this new "family" reality.

If, on the other hand, you are the dependent spouse, this is the time
for you to take a long hard look at your finances. If it has been a while
since you have worked or been responsible for the family money, you'll
need to begin by drawing up a *realistic* budget. Two households simply
cost more than one; there's no way around that. You may find that you
have to be much more frugal than you have been. You may also realize
that you need to go back to work, but be careful—suddenly boosting your
income in the middle of alimony negotiations can dramatically reduce the
amount that you will ultimately receive.

In an ideal world, every couple would simply discuss their respective budgets and agree on an amount, to be paid monthly without question or hassle, from one to the other. Unfortunately, this world of divorce law is far from ideal, and rarely is the question of alimony settled so peacefully. A skilled mediator or collaborative law practitioner can help take a good deal of the acrimony out of the environment, but many couples are unwilling or unable to work within the boundaries of neutrality and compromise. For some, opposing attorneys (who often have good working relationships outside of the context of a case) can function more as go-betweens than as adversaries, but for others, the only way to resolve the issues is to involve a judge. If you find that you have reached this point, remember that both sides will have to prove whatever they claim—if he says he doesn't earn enough to be able to afford a $2000 per month payment, she will need to prove that he can. The need for evidence can result in a protracted process that will drain everyone, both financially and emotionally. Remember, too, that any subsequent adjustments to the court order will require reopening the case, and going back to court.

If, in spite of your (and your attorney's) best efforts, you wind up relying on court-ordered financial support, you may also find yourself relying on the court's ability to enforce that order. The laws vary somewhat from state to state, but generally, failure to pay alimony is considered contempt of court (failing to obey the order issued by the judge), and the threat of potential jail time is what usually guarantees payment. In the long run, though, alimony is rarely a permanent solution to the challenges of dividing one household into two.

# Child Custody: Learning a New Way of Parenting

Of all the issues involved in divorce, child custody is usually the most emotionally charged. Even so, in almost all cases, couples are able to compromise on custody without forcing this issue into court. In many families ne parent has been the primary caregiver throughout the child's life; and the parties agree that this caregiver should continue to have the child most of the time.

Custody decisions should not be, and most often no longer are, a battle to choose one parent to dominate child rearing. Instead, parents should develop a parenting plan to allocate child-rearing responsibilities that can be adapted to meet the changing needs of their children as they mature.

In this chapter we explain the common custody arrangements. We then emphasize the importance of maintaining control of your custody arrangement by reaching agreement with your spouse outside of court. Even for those who don't go to court, understanding the factors judges use in deciding custody is useful as many of those factors make sense to consider when creating your own agreement. An extended discussion of each custody option follows. In the discussion we endeavor to alert you to the issues to as you work to come to agreement on a parenting plan that works best for your family. Finally, we provide you with guidance on how to make your agreement flexible enough to handle changes in circumstances including the possibility that you or your spouse want to move away.

# Child Custody Options

The emotional stress of dealing with child custody is exacerbated by its terminology. To many people, the word "custody" brings to mind property ownership or jail. Others think of classic win/lose custody battles they may have seen in movies. To make matters worse, the parent without custody is given "visitation." This gives the impression that the noncustodial parent is not fully involved with or responsible for the child. While these are the terms used in the laws of most states, if you create an agreement with your spouse regarding the care of your children you can use whatever terms you like.

Child custody has two components. The first, *physical custody*, deals with where the children will live. The second, *legal custody*, addresses who will make the major decisions affecting the children.

There are several options for allocating physical and legal custody. People who wind up in court over custody make it clear that they don't get along very well. Judges tend to assume that these couples will have trouble working together to the degree necessary to share custody so they have traditionally decided to give one parent *sole custody*. That parent has both physical and legal custody of the children. While the children may spend a majority of their time with the custodial parent, it is extremely rare that the noncustodial parent does not have at least the right to visitation. As we'll see later, even visitation schedules that at first seem meager can end up representing 20 to 40 percent of the time a parent might spend with their child in an intact family.

While a parenting arrangement usually specifies a single primary residence for the children (physical custody), decision-making may be shared in an arrangement called *joint legal custody*. The decisions affected by this type of custody include where the children will go to school, how and by whom their medical care will be handled, and what church they will attend. The conventional wisdom is that a parent who does not have physical custody but is included in decision-making will stay more involved with their children. The involvement of noncustodial parents is a key goal of the state because it enhances the child's welfare.

Another option is the sharing of decision-making and physical custody in an arrangement called *joint physical custody*. In this arrangement the children have two primary addresses and switch between them in intervals as short as every few days or as long as every other year. One of the more confusing aspects of custody terminology is that the amount of time a parent has with their children in something termed a joint physical custody arrangement could actually be less than in a sole custody arrangement. None of the options define the percentage of time spent with each parent. This is a very important point because couples often get unnecessarily caught up in fights about terminology when it comes to custody.

Joint physical custody is increasingly used in cases nationwide. The rise in dual income households and the increasing involvement of fathers in raising their kids are contributing to the growth of this arrangement. In dual income households where both parents have demanding work schedules, a sole custody arrangement requiring one spouse to be responsible for the bulk of the parenting time can diminish the quality of the care that parent can provide. Joint custody balances the load.

Many states, including Florida and Texas, have laws that specify that joint physical and legal custody is preferred or to be presumed. An additional group of states indicate a similar preference or presumption if the parents agree on joint custody, thus reducing the chances that a judge's preference for sole custody would override the parents' wishes. A judge could still order sole custody but might be required to document the reasons for doing so. The presence of domestic violence, drug addiction, or similarly threatening situations will almost certainly result in a judge deviating from a state's preference for joint custody.

The problems with the terminology of child custody have been recognized by most experts. Legislatures have started to use new terminology that you may encounter. *Primary custody* is essentially a synonym for sole custody but better reflects that sole custody does not eliminate the involvement on the other parent. *Parenting time* is replacing visitation and reduces the stigma associated with labeling a parent as simply a visitor. *Shared parenting* refers to a sole custody or joint custody arrangement in which the child spends at least one third of the time with each parent.

Legal custody is being replaced with the clearer phrase *decision-making responsibility*. Physical custody is becoming *residential time.*

The final term we will introduce is *parenting plan*. This is a written agreement that specifies how you will handle decision making responsibility, residential arrangements and parenting time. Some plans address the financial aspects of raising the children (covered in the next chapter). The plan should address how future disagreements will be resolved, whether there will be periodic reviews of the plan, and how it will be modified. Typically, court approval of the plan is required.

---

# Avoid a Custody Battle

If you have a shattered relationship with your spouse and you feel you will be unable to resolve all of the issues of your divorce outside of court, focus your efforts on trying to agree on custody first. A courtroom custody fight should be avoided if at all possible. Make sure you consider the options presented later in this book for resolving your dispute outside of court. Having a court decide on custody is likely to be costly, emotionally draining, embarrassing, unpredictable, and may result in a solution that is less than ideal for your family. If that weren't enough, parental conflict over children has significant negative effects on the kids. Aside from the initial court fight, an inflexible, court-imposed custody order can lead to ongoing conflict.

Having a judge decide custody is costly because not only will you generally require an attorney to represent you, but one or more experts may also be required by the court or recommended by your attorney to perform a custody evaluation. In some areas these evaluations can cost tens of thousands of dollars. And, although the couple pays for the expert, the expert is independent and won't necessarily present an opinion that matches the wishes of either parent.

Custody court cases are emotionally draining and embarrassing because your private life is on display in a public courtroom. Anything you may have done in your past that might reflect on your character, or any mental health issues you may have now or have had in the past will be fair game for the other side to drag out.

The unpredictability and limited quality of results of custody trials is due to a number of factors. You usually have little or no control over which judge will hear your case. Judges may have biases that come from dated notions about custody. They don't usually have the opportunity to see the long-term effects of their custody decisions and are not required to read or utilize research on such matters in making their decisions. In some jurisdictions, judges rotate duties, or inexperienced judges are assigned to hear family court cases. These situations make it difficult for any judge to be an expert in evaluating what will be best for the child. Of course, there are many great judges who can be trusted to make wise decisions. However, you cannot guarantee that you will get one of those.

The amount of time a judge can take to make a decision in a custody trial is limited. This, coupled with the reticence most judges feel about making custody decisions, has led to the increasing reliance on outside experts. A custody evaluator may be appointed by the court to interview the family, babysitters, teachers, and others. An evaluator may administer psychological tests to parents and children. Evaluators are supposed to limit their work to gauging the parties' "parenting capacity" and how that fits the psychological needs of the child. However, many evaluators, often at the urging of judges, expand the role significantly. Evaluators frequently create detailed recommendations for parenting plans, which are likely to be accepted by the judge. There are few rules about how custody evaluators should perform their work and few procedures for complaining if a parent believes the evaluator got it wrong. The lack of studies to support the life altering conclusions developed by evaluators is a cause for concern, even for some evaluators.

Finally, your child's developmental changes or special needs will likely result in your wanting changes in your parenting schedule. The only way to achieve a flexible schedule that is able to grow and change with your children's lives is through agreement.

# Courtroom Custody Decisions

Some couples are unable to agree on how to handle custody and must go to court to resolve the matter. Others initially agree, but issues arise that they are unable to settle. Many couples decide to settle only after getting an understanding of what a court custody fight is really like. For these reasons, it is useful for all couples to understand what happens when a judge must make a custody decision.

When deciding a custody case, the court's primary focus is on creating an arrangement that is "in the best interests of the child." Unfortunately, although this is the usual legal standard, it is a nebulous concept that allows for a great deal of argument. The arrangement should assure the child's health, safety, and welfare. Some states consider frequent and continuing contact with both parents to be in the best interest of the child, as long as there is no history of abuse. This has led many courts to prefer joint custody or, if not, then a sole custody arrangement with generous visitation. However, there is no conclusive long-term proof of what form of custody works best. Legislative preferences vary from state to state. Even when the state declares a preference in its statutes, the individual nature of each case gives judges great leeway to exercise their own preferences.

In court, the focus on the best interests of the child in determining with whom your child will reside forces the court to direct its attention principally to you and your spouse. The court, therefore, will carefully examine your conduct in the past to predict how you will behave in the future. The trial judge is given wide discretion in his or her determination. Appellate review is very limited in this kind of litigation as the courts of appeal are unwilling to substitute their judgment of the facts, since the trial judge was the one who reviewed all of the evidence presented.

Although your child's welfare is the focus of the proceeding, your child may or may not participate in the court process. The judge and your lawyers may all agree that appearing in court might be unduly traumatic for your child or that he or she might not understand what was expected.

In some cases the judge may talk with your child in chambers. Lawyers may be present, but not parents. This is intended to allow the child to speak more freely. A private, in-chambers (*in camera*) interview helps the judge better understand the child and the parent-child relationship.

In cases involving older children the judge may inquire directly or indirectly about the child's preferences regarding custody. Indirect questioning might involve asking about how the child spends time with each parent and what he or she likes to do best with each. The older the child, the more impact preference is likely to have on the judge. Usually a judge will factor in the opinion of a child aged ten or twelve on up.

One aspect of custody cases that may be surprising is that the rules regarding the burden of proof and other rules of evidence may be relaxed. Judges may rely on evidence that would be inadmissible in a criminal trial. They may also become more involved in gathering the details they need to make a decision. Thus, the divorce process might see the judge assuming a more inquisitorial role than in other types of cases.

As stated earlier, judges sometimes rely on custody evaluators to help them get a better understanding of the family than can be obtained during a fairly quick trial. Keep in mind that while judges or custody evaluators are expected to be wise and all-knowing, they may be unable to easily relate to your family and the information provided. The custody decision is very personal. It's hard for a stranger to really understand how the family works and what custody options would fit best.

Judges generally have wide discretion in the factors they consider when making custody decisions, and how much weight they give to each. The judge may consider the following:

- The parenting plan each parent wants.
- All things that might impinge on the development of the child's physical, mental, emotional, moral, and spiritual faculties. In considering the child's developmental needs, the judge would take a child's age into account.
- Each parent's history and capacities as a caregiver.
- The home environment that each parent could provide to the child.

- The time available to each parent to be with the child, as the judge may wish to maximize the child's time with a parent as opposed to a babysitter or daycare center. The judge will want to know current and future work and travel schedules.
- The child's bonding with each parent and with other siblings, if there are any.
- Parental involvement in school, extracurricular, or religious activities.
- Either parent's plan to or likelihood of moving away.
- The child's preference, although this is not required.
- The presence of current or past mental instability in either parent.
- Current or past alcohol or drug abuse.
- Any physical problems that could prevent the parent from adequately taking care of the child.
- Parent's history of cooperating with the other parent or, on the other hand, undermining the relationship between the child and the other parent by actions such as interfering with visitation or cutting off phone contact.
- Parent's involvement in adulterous relationship or dating.
- Any history of domestic violence or sexual abuse. Such a history generally results in more stringent rules relating to how the judge decides the case.

Even though parents may each state their desire for sole custody of the children, the judge may decide to split custody in ways that please neither side. Parents in a bitter divorce often want to deny the former spouse access to their children. It is important, though, to recognize that judges are rarely swayed by the adult nastiness. Even in cases of domestic violence, the judge is likely to recognize the abusive parent's right to maintain a relationship with his or her child. In such cases, the judge may limit the parent's visits and/or require supervision by a third party, but don't assume that just because your ex is a jerk the judge will deny visitation.

# Courtroom Secrets

During the course of our many years of trying custody cases, we have learned a great deal about how to make the system work to achieve what our client believes is in the best interest of their child. A lot of that knowledge is legal skill that you will need to rely on your lawyer to employ on your behalf. However, there are a few things you can do that we have seen work particularly well in custody cases. Make use of these tips, and you might get the edge you need to prevail if you wind up in court.

The first secret is that judges are bored by testimony about who brushes your child's teeth, tucks them in, attends their games, and takes them to the doctor. This is what family court judges hear day in and day out. Your objective is to stand out in a positive way so the judge gives your side's presentation more of his attention. What works here is using pictures, videotapes, and items from school like cards and letters, etc. These visually interesting items have a much greater impact than someone's voice alone. They help the judge personalize your relationship with your child. We recommend that as you identify items that may have value to your case, store them in your lawyer's office or at a friend's house. Don't hide them in your own home, especially if your spouse is still there. Treat these items with extreme care as they could wind up being crucial to your case.

The second secret relates to being recognized as a good parent. Everyone knows the conundrum, "If a tree falls in a forest and no one is there to hear it, does it make a sound?" Our version goes, "If you are a great parent and nobody knows it, are you a great parent?" Every custody case involves differences of opinion about the fitness of the other parent. Each parent highlights his or her own parental abilities and brings out the shortcomings of the other spouse. The judge must rely on witnesses to paint a more objective picture of the parents. The witnesses who make a difference are the people who see you parent your children. Here are some examples:

- A day care teacher who sees the excitement of your child when you arrive for pickup.

- A nurse at your pediatrician's office who recalls that you are always there when your child is sick.
- A neighbor who sees you playing catch outside after work.
- Relatives who know about your parenting.

The bottom line is, don't be an invisible parent. If you are a great parent who hasn't been visible, you can correct the situation. If you are thinking about being in court, you will probably have a lot of time to prepare—usually six months, a year or more. You can use that time to be visibly involved with your child in the presence of people who can support your case.

Third, the person who can give the most specific examples to illustrate his or her case is generally deemed to be more credible. We advise our clients to keep a journal of everything that happens related to the ex-spouse and the children. Record items like when your child was returned after visitation, what your spouse said when returning the child, anything you notice about child care (such as improper clothing at school or illness). The journal is important, because you won't be able to remember specifics six months down the road. The only downside to this suggestion is that it can make it harder to come to agreement later, because you have become focused on noticing the negatives about the way your spouse is handling parenting responsibilities. Of course, you could also record the positives which, although we have yet to see it, could help you see your spouse in a different light and be helpful in finding agreement. As with all the other issues of contention that we're covering, you could view this as an exercise in improving your relationship and parenting skills. Growth is good, right?

Another option is recording telephone conversations with your spouse and keeping voicemail recordings from him or her. These recordings might be used in court if it is necessary to show that the other parent is hostile or abusive, or to prove admissions that he or she might make outside of court about the care of the child. Tape recordings help eliminate the general he said/she said arguments that occur in custody trials. Be cautious, though; while taping is legal in most states when at least one person consents, there are some states where this is not the case. Reporters Committee is a website designed for reporters, but equally useful for parents, has state-by-state information about the legalities of recording conversations. Some parents secretly tape conversations between their child and their former spouse. This is generally illegal and is not advised.

Finally, it's clear to us that what most judges are looking for when presiding over a custody case is a parent who can be trusted to take care of the child. While it's important to not allow the other side to steamroll you, avoiding over-the-top allegations that diminish your credibility can help create the impression that you are responsible and can be trusted.

## The Real-World Impact of Custody Choices

Hopefully we've convinced you that having a judge decide custody for you is to be avoided if at all possible. The question now is what custody arrangement makes the most sense for your family. As you read more about each custody option you will best be able to determine what fits. In a later section we'll cover the obstacles you might come up against in getting agreement, and provide suggestions for how you might get around them.

How do different custody options affect children? The late Judith Wallerstein, a respected divorce researcher and author, wrote in her book *What About the Kids?* that "there is no scientific evidence that the general psychological adjustment of children is related to any particular form of custody." Her studies, and others, indicate that "the amount time spent with either parent is not relevant to the child's well-being." She has found that the factors that are relevant to the child's adjustment are:

- The child's psychological health.
- Each parent's psychological health.
- The quality of the relationship between the child and each parent.
- The quality of the parents' relationship with each other.

Wallerstein's conclusions make sense when we consider that we often maintain stronger relationships with distant parents, siblings or friends than we do with the people we see every day. Though they may seem like common sense, her conclusions are not without controversy. A study published in the *Journal of Family Psychology* by Robert Bauserman concludes that children in joint custody were better adjusted than those in sole custody. Unfortunately, no large-scale, long-term studies exist in this area at this time.

In the absence of conclusive research, separate fathers' (or, more gender neutrally "separated parents") and mothers' rights movements promote the research that best serves their independent causes and attempt to debunk the rest. As in most political debates, the groups generally choose to cast each other's positions as extreme. One side argues against children going to court with two parents and leaving with only one. The other argues against rigid, arbitrary 50/50 splits of parenting time that are disruptive and damaging to children. The fact is that courts rarely impose either of these extremes. While the advocates may have roles to play in focusing policy-makers' attention on child custody issues, it is important to not get caught up in their ongoing debate. Maintain your focus on forming an agreement that works best for your family.

An important consideration when developing a custody agreement is what will keep both parents involved with the children. Regardless of what an agreement or court order says, nothing can force a parent to be involved in a child's life. Even a noncustodial parent who fought for a large amount of visitation may later drift away. There is no requirement that any parent actually exercise visitation rights. Recognizing this reality, it's important to consider how to best structure your parenting plan to maintain involvement, and to realize that making the plan work as designed will require an ongoing commitment from both parents.

The primary advantage of sole custody, particularly the residential aspect of it, is that it provides a single, stable home environment. Kids appreciate being able to stay with one set of friends, especially if they are fortunate enough to remain in the marital residence and maintain their existing neighborhood friends. Many kids are involved in activities, like athletics, near the home can become difficult to manage if they are frequently away from the area.

The biggest problems with sole custody are related to the challenges it creates in maintaining the involvement of both parents in the child's life. When a noncustodial parent's responsibilities and time are limited, he/she may feel less connected with his child. These parents have to work hard to figure out how to maintain special connections with their children, given their limited time together. They can often use phone or email outside of the times they are with their children to extend the connection. Parents are wise not to overdo it though. It's important to remember that sometimes kids want to be with their friends or play with a new toy more than spending time with either parent. That's just natural.

Some noncustodial parents have trouble making their limited parenting time work. They may feel uncomfortable carving out a fully formed role in the children's lives. Are they there just to provide entertainment? Some parents may feel more like weekend babysitters relieving the child's "real" parent rather than an integral part of the child's life. This can become even more acute if the custodial parent has remarried. What works will be very individual, and will often require the support of the custodial parent. Just like in intact families, children should spend time with divorced parents engaging in a mix of fun and mundane activities, ranging from hanging out to doing chores.

Another challenge of sole custody that should not be minimized is the burden it places on the parent with primary custody. It is common after divorce for that parent to not only have to handle considerably more childcare without assistance but to also deal with reentering the workforce or going to school to enhance earning ability. The net result can be that kids end up spending more time in day care or with sitters.

In divorced families with joint physical custody the child has two homes and divides his or her time between them. The major benefit in this arrangement is the way it structurally encourages the maintenance of a relationship between the children and each parent. Of course, such relationships aren't guaranteed, and a forced joint custody arrangement where one parent cares deeply about the children and the other truly has other interests, can do more harm than good.

Another benefit of joint physical custody is the time it provides for each parent to be without the children. In the two career households where joint custody is most common, this freedom allows some parents to focus on career enhancement. Others use the time for socializing or dating. The only stress comes in the potential difficulty of changing gears from being someone with more freedom back to being a full-time parent.

Kids in joint physical custody arrangements also may have difficult shifting between houses. Being in constant transit between houses can get old. Kids can get confused about which house to go to after school. Depending on the kids' ages, you may need to figure out some system of reminders--perhaps a big calendar or a tag sent each day to school to eliminate this concern from your child's days. Older kids can get frustrated with moving between homes when they forget to bring a school book or assignment they need, or a piece of clothing they were planning to wear.

Joint physical custody is an expensive arrangement, which explains why it occurs more frequently in upper income families. Kids need dedicated space in each home. They shouldn't be put in a situation where they are kicking a parent or another person out of bed when they are present. Within reason, their space should also be protected so they feel that things they leave during one stay at the house will still be there when they return. This typically becomes more of an issue when a parent remarries and stepchildren are present.

Joint custody requires more communication between spouses. This can be difficult for couples that are still angry. The communication is required, because children need consistency in things like rules, bedtimes, and diet. Without that consistency, the world can seem confusing, causing kids to develop discipline problems (or worse).

Making and maintaining friends in two neighborhoods can be an overwhelming challenge for some kids. They may end up feeling lonely in one home or the other. Parents can help their children meet neighbors, but there's no guarantee—the neighborhood kids may or may not accept a part-time resident into their group the way they would a new permanent family. Prior to the arrival of your child in a new neighborhood, do some groundwork by exploring the area. Then when your child arrives, show him or her around; you can work together to get comfortable in the new environment.

Shared custody arrangements have proven to be less stable than sole custody arrangements. Over time, about a third of these plans drift into formal or de facto sole custody arrangements for a variety of reasons. Making joint custody succeed requires time and effort in maintaining communication and coordinating schedules. Parents must organize their lives to support the arrangement, including maintaining residences reasonably close to each other. The relationship between divorced parents needs to be relatively amicable. The old relationship obviously had serious problems that led to the divorce—you will need to be able to work together to support the development of your children. If parents continue to fight after divorce, especially over issues relating to the custody arrangement, the children can have great difficulty adjusting to life after divorce.

Most successful joint custody arrangements occur when both parents were significantly engaged in the parenting during the marriage. Where there has been significantly more caretaking by one parent than the other, entering into a joint custody arrangement can lead to instability in the child's life as roles change. It is important for anyone advocating joint custody to be certain that both parties are willing to accept the responsibility that it entails.

Although it is rare, some parents have found success with a concept called "nesting," where instead of the children moving between homes, they stay in one home, and the parents move in and out based on a schedule. This type of arrangement requires a great deal of coordination and cooperation, and can be hard to maintain, especially if one parent remarries. However, the advantage of maintaining consistency for the children may outweigh the inconvenience to the parents.

## Listening to the Children

We have already discussed the role of children's preferences in courtroom custody fights. But what if you are developing an agreement outside of court? How do you incorporate your child's desires into your thinking without putting too much pressure on them?

First of all, it is important to step back and remember that children *need* adults to guide them in all areas of their lives. When asked, children going through a divorce will overwhelmingly say they want joint custody, but the vast majority of children have little real understanding of the long-term issues of life in a divided household.

Wallerstein emphasizes the importance of listening to the children, but not giving them a veto. She writes about the fear children have of being forgotten; the things that provide them comfort may be surprising. It is important to give children time and emotional space in which to adjust to this new reality, but it is equally important, now more than ever, to be a parent.

As harsh as this may sound, we don't believe that young children should be able to decide when they will see their parents. Yes, all children should be allowed some input into the direction of their lives. But they don't decide whether they go to school, the doctor, or the dentist. They don't decide their vacation spot for the summer. They don't decide who their child care provider will be, or even whether they will receive child care. So likewise, they don't decide when and if they will see their parents. Nor do they decide under what conditions. In fact, a child may seem puzzled if asked his or her opinion. Do their feelings and emotions matter? Of course they do. But a child's emotions do not dictate everything that happens to him or her. Adults still make those choices, and if parents can't agree, then a judge in a courtroom will have to make the decisions for them. In a courtroom a child's feelings may be heard, but in the end the judge decides, not the child.

## Reaching Agreement

No custody arrangement works as well as an intact family. Inevitably there is some loss as a result of the divorce. Every arrangement has benefits and drawbacks for each family member. While everyone's concerns need to be considered, parents need to maintain their focus on what is in the best interests of the children.

When a parent fails to maintain focus on the best interests of the children, things can go from bad to worse very quickly. Parents who reach an agreement without focusing on their children's interests risk having the agreement challenged later, and the court will maintain an interest in the children's welfare until they are adults.

While the prospect of being subjected to the dictate of a judge can be frightening, we urge you to remember that most people are able to reach agreement without ever going to court. Even if you are being threatened with court, it is best if you focus your energy on creating an agreement that works for your family rather than on worrying too much about what would happen in court.

People make poor decisions under stress, and especially when they are threatened with the loss of their children. If you are the one under stress take your time in the negotiation process. If you are having trouble with anger or fear and can't get past it, remember to rely on the support system we wrote about earlier in the book. Whatever you do, don't be pressured into making a decision you can't live with or feel won't work out. Sometimes an attorney will say that you should accept something in your agreement because, based on experience, he or she expects that things will change in your favor later. That scenario may be right in *almost* all cases, but you must make sure you can live with the consequences if your case proves to be the exception. While you and your spouse can change your agreement later, if you can't agree to the change, you might have to go to court to prove that the change was in the child's best interest.

In court custody fights, a parent can bolster a position by focusing on the spouse's weaknesses. This is obviously harmful to the ongoing relationship of two people who are trying to raise children in tandem. When parents work together to create their own parenting plan, they will improve their chances of success if they turn their attention to each other's strengths. This focus enables them to think of the benefits each parent can provide the children to meet developmental needs. Working together this way reduces hostility and begins your new relationship as separated parents. The process of creating your agreement can be difficult, but can ultimately help each of you develop the communication skills you will need to effectively and cooperatively parent throughout your children's lives. If you really want to do what's best for your kids, you simply have no choice but to find a way to work together with the other person who is responsible for the children you both love.

# Scheduling Parenting Time

In reaching agreement you will focus on the time each of you spends with the kids and the control of decision-making. We'll first focus on the issue of dividing the time. You or one of the attorneys will write your decisions into a divorce agreement or parenting plan. In your parenting plan you can usually use whatever terms you like to describe your arrangement, bearing in mind that terms like noncustodial parent and visitation are often contentious. In the following discussion we'll stay away from these terms and consider the case of two parents, Sam and Terry, and assume that the parent who will provide the bulk of the caretaking will be Sam who is a stay at home parent.

The most common schedule we see both parents and judges arrive at is for the child to live with "Sam" and spend alternating weekends and one or two weeknights for dinner or an overnight with "Terry." Holiday periods are alternated: for instance, Christmas one year, Thanksgiving the next. School breaks may also be alternated. Summer vacation is split, with the child spending anywhere from one week to six weeks with dad.

We have already discussed how research shows that the amount of time spent by each parent with a child is not relevant to the child's well-being. However, we've rarely found a parent willing to accept this conclusion. Many parents get very hung up on the exact amount of time.

At first glance, "Terry" might think the generic schedule allows very limited time with the children. What we often do is go through the exact hours together, taking into account the work and school schedules of the child and parent. What comes to light is that even in an intact family, when "Terry" works a typical schedule, the amount of time spent seeing the kids in the morning and in the evening (between arrival home and bedtime) is relatively small. Being away from the child on four out of five school nights doesn't tip the balance as much as might be expected. Depending on your schedules, you might find something along the lines of a sixty/forty split in waking time with your child.

If you are a parent seeking more time with your children than the standard schedule provides, there are a number of options you can ask for that can help achieve your goals:

- Ask to be able to keep the child during any holidays connected to your weekends. Aside from national and state holidays, schools have regular teacher workdays, which parents are often willing to accept as part of a long weekend with whichever parent is on the schedule for that time.

- Extend your weekend time together from ending on Sunday night to ending on Monday morning, in order to get another night and morning together.

- Give yourself right of first refusal when the parent on the schedule needs a babysitter. This means that they will be required to see if you are available and interested in taking the kids, instead of bringing in someone else. While the amount of time this involves is hard to predict, it could be substantial.

- Use the many weeks available in the summer to make up for lost time during the school year. Summers are obviously great times for a trip together, where you can focus your attention on your child and together you can build lasting memories. The challenge with summer, of course, is that kids need something to do, and parents usually need to work.

If you find yourself fighting to get one or two extra overnights per month, consider giving in. You may be pleasantly surprised, down the road, to find that you get the extra overnight anyway, as the reality of full-time parenting sets in and your ex-spouse's life evolves.

Parents with more than one child can consider sharing transportation duties in the evenings. Often the kids will participate in activities with schedules that are nearly impossible for one parent to manage alone. A parent looking for ways to spend more time with his or her children could handle driving one child to or from an event, which helps everyone.

This transportation concept works really well with older kids, who, we're sorry to say, often aren't very interested in time with parents. They prefer to spend time with friends. Fighting about the amount of time you get with your older child may lead to disappointment. However, we've learned that one of the best times for parents to talk to teenagers is when they're in the car together. Instead of asking for more overnights, consider the creative solution of being the one to drive them wherever they need to go. It doesn't sound like much fun, but it may be the best way to stay connected with a teen.

As you can now see, the parenting schedule, even in a sole custody arrangement, can result in a much more even division of parenting time than might have first been expected. When parents focus on this reality instead of preconceived notions or semantic subtleties, a lot of the emotion around these negotiations can fade away. Parents can then stop fighting about hours, and instead consider their children's needs and the creation of a parenting plan that works well for the kids.

---

## Matching Schedules and Children

The research regarding the effects of different parenting schedules on children is inconclusive. Even if the research was in place and states incorporated it into guidelines, the individual characteristics of each child would be lost. Especially when children are under about age six (school age), you need to make sure that the parenting plan takes into account the child's individual needs. If you have more than one child, and one or more is young, you will probably need work out separate, child-specific schedules with your spouse.

It is not recommended that overnights be scheduled for children under a year. The change in environment and prolonged detachment from the primary caregiver can be traumatic. However, the child's other parent is encouraged to visit frequently and predictably. As kids grow, their tolerance for overnight stays increases. Overnights in the second and third year should limited. The child's reaction should guide both parents regarding whether the arrangement is developmentally appropriate. Experts don't recommend consecutive overnights until the child is three.

When considering a parenting schedule for each child, parents need to consider a number of questions:

- Where is the child developmentally?
- How well does the child separate from the primary caregiver?
- Has he or she ever spent the night without that person, and how did that go?
- How sensitive is the child to changes in the environment?

Honest answers to these questions will help you work together to identify a reasonable schedule that will most benefit the child. When creating schedules for your young children, you can map out the schedule agreed upon once the child becomes more mature (perhaps age 6). In the interim, you will need to work together periodically to move from an initial plan to the final schedule.

# Decision-Making

The other area that needs to be addressed when developing a parenting agreement is decision making. Obviously, the parent who is with the child makes the bulk of immediate decisions, such as whether the child can go to a movie, buy something, or visit a friend. In most cases this is not an issue, and there really isn't an alternative. Nobody would put up with micromanagement of these issues from afar. Parents will need to trust each other's judgment and, where they find the former spouse's parenting style is leading to trouble, must discuss the issue. It's impossible to use a legal agreement to control all of the decisions parents need to make, although such an agreement can establish parameters and preferences to use as reference in future discussions. If you both agree now that TV should be limited until the children are older, and you put that in your agreement, you can remind your spouse of the agreement if you need to raise the issue later.

Determining how *major* decisions will be made for children can become a real sticking point for some parents. These decisions usually relate to education, healthcare, and religion. One important thing to consider about these decisions is that there aren't really very many of them. Also, most couples shared many values when they were married. Fighting over the right to make decisions that would likely be made in the same way by your former spouse anyway is counter-productive. On the other hand, parents who are left out of decision-making may feel less inclined to be involved with their children overall. For that reason, we feel that it is crucial, for the well-being of your children, that you find a way to *share* the big decisions with your ex.

If your marriage has involved a lot of conflict, and you feel that shared decision-making may not work, consider planning for this in your agreement by incorporating alternative dispute resolution options such as mediation, followed by arbitration. This approach can avoid the cost of going to court and help get the decision made quickly enough to still be relevant.

## Information Sharing

Generally, information about health and education must be provided to a noncustodial parent, with few exceptions. State statutes do vary somewhat in their specificity regarding the exact documents to be provided. It is valuable in maintaining the child's relationship with both parents to ensure that both parents are equally informed about the child.

Your parenting plan needs to consider what information about the children will be shared by the parents, and how. You will likely want to include some text broadening the type of information shared from the minimum the state may require. For instance, game schedules and school performances should be included, but these daily details will not necessarily be specified by a court agreement.

It is improper to burden children with the job of transmitting information from one parent to the other. If it is later claimed that information is not being provided, a judge will be displeased if a parent blames a child for the omission. Our advice is for the parent who gets these records to provide them to the other parent without being asked. This eliminates a common source of frustration between separated parents. There are now online tools designed for divorced parents that allow one parent to post information in a place where the other can access it at any time.

These tools can even record when the information was posted, in case a dispute comes up later regarding the timeliness of information sharing.

If problems do arise, one simple solution may be for the nonresidential parent to get duplicate information directly from the source. For instance, teachers are now accustomed to dealing with children with separated parents, and can often provide two copies of everything they send home.

## Grandparents and Others

State laws provide grandparents with rights to visit their grandchildren. Rather than relying on legal status, though, it's best for both parties to consider the children's grandparents, extended family members (aunts, uncles, cousins), and other important adults, when creating their parenting plan. The plan might provide for children to periodically visit distant grandparents, or for the grandparents to see the children when they are in town. The opportunity for a child to have a relationship with a loving adult from another generation can be invaluable. Similarly, visits with cousins can build life-long relationships of which children of divorce should not be deprived.

## Allow for Changes

Since more than 50 percent of divorced people remarry, you can assume that your (or your former spouse's) life may change, and that such changes could affect the way you parent your children. At the same time, kids grow and develop in unexpected ways, and may benefit from different amounts of time with different parents. Household schedules can change, so a drop-off or pick-up time that once was carefully placed before or after dinner doesn't work anymore because the evening plan was shifted to accommodate swimming or band practice.

The ideal situation for a parenting agreement is that you never really have to refer to it again, because through the process of creating the document you have formed a new relationship with your former spouse that allows you to work things out. You don't want to have to go back to the contract to handle every change that occurs in your lives. The agreement should really act as a safety net. It catches you if you can't work things out on your own.

When creating your parenting plan, recognize that your children will grow and change. Unless you are a very new parent at the time of your divorce, you know already that children change dramatically as they proceed through developmental milestones on the way to adulthood. Parents also know that each child brings his or her own surprises along the way. Wise parents agree to meet monthly, quarterly, or, at the very least, twice yearly, to talk about how their children are doing. A half-hour conference over coffee every few months can go a long way toward preventing future disagreements.

Some parents write into their agreement that they will reevaluate it at specific intervals, perhaps based on certain developmental milestones. This helps set the expectation that parents may need to consider whether or not to modify the plan to meet the child's new needs. While parents just getting through stressful negotiations about parenting or other aspects of their divorce may expect future meetings to be similarly challenging, let us assure you that in most cases it gets easier, not harder, to agree as time passes.

If you need to tweak your parenting plan over the years, you don't need to sign new documents or go to court. You, as parents, will hopefully develop your new parenting relationship and proceed through the myriad of issues to raise your child together. There is less risk involved in agreeing to informal changes in parenting arrangements (as opposed to child support), because there is no retroactivity to court decisions relating to custody. In other words, if a court modifies your parenting schedule at some point, it is unlikely that you will have to "give back" time that you've already spent with the child.

If a couple finds that they are running into unforeseen problems that they can't resolve, they can bring in a third party (such as a mediator) to help. They may even wish to specify in the agreement that an arbitrator will be used if necessary. Regardless of what the agreement says, if the result of any process used to make a decision that affects the child is not in the best interests of the child, the issue can be taken to a judge.

# Moving

The United States is a mobile society. People move for work, to be closer to other family members, or to simply start a new life. As you can imagine, the desire of one parent to move can be troublesome when it comes to child custody. Having children results in a loss of freedom in general, and the ability to move is a freedom that may be affected even after a divorce. The battles that ensue when a parent with custody moves away with the children are some of the fiercest in family law.

When couples fight about a move, both sides argue that their position is based on the best interests of the child. The parent wanting the move usually says that a job opportunity available elsewhere will enhance the child's life. The parent staying put says that the children are best off staying where they can have two involved parents.

The legal waters regarding the rights of custodial parents to move are murky. It has traditionally been the case that the custodial parent has broad discretion to make decisions for children including where they will live. What was best for that parent was thought to be best for the child.

A recent California Supreme Court decision in a move-away case resulted in a mother's loss of her children because she moved. This doesn't mean that all, or even most, custodial parents would be prevented from moving, but such a decision in California is likely to have effects in other states.

The California decision gave judges broader discretion to make decisions for divorced families. The factors that a judge may include when considering a voluntary move include the stability and continuity in the custody arrangement, the relationships of both parents with the children and with each other, the distance of and reasons for the move, and the children's wishes. One net effect of the decision may be that parents are discouraged from even trying to move. Although we recognize the argument that a custodial parent should have a right to live where he or she pleases, in general we feel that when the best interests of the child are honestly considered, it is best for the parents to stay in a location where they can both be regularly and continuously involved with their children.

If you feel that you might need or want to move at some point in time, you can help ensure your right to do so by being a good parent and fostering your child's relationship with the other parent. Attempts to interfere with that relationship can have negative effects in court. If you are concerned about your spouse moving, you can add provisions into your agreement requiring him or her to provide you with ample notification, so that you can work out a new parenting plan, or even take the matter to court if necessary. You can also agree to limit the timing of such moves so that they don't occur in the middle of school years. Ultimately, your agreement may be overridden by a judge, but only if one of you forces the issue. Because the courts can intervene in the case of a move, and may even be required to at least approve the move, it is usually inadvisable to block an agreement just because you cannot agree about provisions relating to moving.

# Child Support: Caring for and Anticipating Needs

Divorce does not end your responsibility to care for your children. Most parents acknowledge this fundamental concept, and genuinely wish to provide for their children. These positive feelings make the negotiation of child support one of the least contentious issues in divorce. That said, it still takes work to agree on the specifics of child support. The more you understand about the issues before you begin negotiations, the more likely you are to quickly achieve a fair agreement.

Child support is typically a monthly payment from the noncustodial parent to the custodial parent to provide for the needs of the couple's children. Although the maintenance of two households will result in higher living expenses for both you and your former spouse, child support helps to ensure that the children's standard of living is not significantly altered by the divorce.

Like child custody agreements, child support determinations are generally long-lasting. A spouse who feels he or she was not treated fairly regarding property division (generally a one-time negotiation) is usually able to get past those feelings as life goes on after the divorce. But child support usually continues until the children are eighteen. A spouse who feels that the amount is unfair might be reminded of this fact every month for more than a decade. Such feelings are not simply painful but, in the payer's case, may result in failure to consistently meet the financial obligation.

The effect of child support arrangements on the relationship between the noncustodial parent and the kids should not be overlooked. If the parent with custody feels strongly that the payments are inadequate, he or she may express that frustration to the children. In this environment, a child's natural disappointment about not being able to have every toy or gadget on the market can turn to blame and resentment directed at the absent parent. Even if the noncustodial parent is paying a substantial portion of his or her income in child support, the feelings surrounding the payments must be considered to avoid such a negative outcome.

## The Challenge of Determining a Fair Amount

Failing to invest the time necessary to understand the true costs of raising your children is likely to result in on-going conflict with your spouse. Our experience is that most people underestimate the true costs involved in raising children. This is partly due to the difficulty most of us have balancing our family budgets month to month. Trying to ferret out which expenses relate to children is an even tougher chore.

Many child-related expenses are obvious and relatively easy to budget; examples include clothing and groceries. Other expenses are more difficult to isolate. Consider the following expenses incurred by the parent with custody:

- Larger house or apartment including bedrooms, play area, and utilities and maintenance expenses.
- Larger car to transport kids and friends.
- Costs associated with time off from work for doctor appointments
- Reduction in potential income due to inability to work or study extra hours to improve employment situation.

Child support payments are rarely enough to cover the costs the custodial parent bears in raising the children.

When one parent has sole custody, expenses relating to children don't rise, but they are hard to identify and agree upon. Parents with shared custody get stretched further, because they have to maintain two households where children can feel comfortable. Aside from the extra space needed to house them, there will be added costs due to the duplication of items like toys and clothes.

Regardless of the type of custody, families simply have fewer resources after divorce than they did before. Parents generally want to maintain the same standard of living for their children, and this concept is supported in the law. The only way to make this happen, though, is for both parents to understand the costs associated with raising their children, and to work together (or through attorneys) to create a budget that achieves their goals and is affordable.

Successfully negotiating child support has many advantages over resorting to a court order. Although child support court orders are not the wildcards they once were, they are usually based on arbitrary formulas that fail to take into account the unique needs of your family, and often result in one or both parents being dissatisfied.

# Child Support Guidelines

Unlike most other aspects of divorce, child support is an area where the federal government has an interest and has become involved. Children who are not adequately cared for add to the strain on the safety net that the federal government funds. After studies revealed serious inconsistencies in the way judges were determining child support, Congress passed laws in the 1980s requiring states to create and use what are known as "child support guidelines." The federal government has also become increasingly involved in the enforcement of child support. Among other things, they have made it possible to withhold portions of employee paychecks and deduct funds from tax refunds to ensure child support is paid.

The goals of the guidelines adopted by the states are generally the same. Tennessee's includes the following list of typical goals:

- To decrease the number of impoverished children living in single parent families.
- To make child support awards more equitable by ensuring more consistent treatment of persons in similar circumstances.

- To improve efficiency of the court process by promoting settlements and by giving courts and parties guidance in establishing level of support awards.
- To encourage parents paying support to maintain contact with their children.
- To ensure that when parents live separately, the economic impact on the children is minimized and to the extent that either parent enjoys a higher standard of living, the children share(s) in that higher standard.
- To ensure that a minimum amount of child support is set for parents with a low income in order to maintain a bond between the parent and the child, to establish patterns of regular payment, and to enable the enforcement agency and party receiving support to maintain contact with the parent paying support.

Congress' effort to improve the consistency of child support was successful in that calculations within a state are consistent. However, since the states maintained control over the implementation of the guidelines there is considerable variation between each state. In general, each state chose to use one of three approaches to determine the amount of child support.

Some states use a "percentage of income" method that determines child support as a percentage of income of just the payer. The percentage to be paid is based on the number of children and, in some states, on the amount of income. There is variation among states as to what items can be deducted from income prior to the calculation. Proponents' rights groups have been fighting against usage of this method because they believe that ignoring the income of the custodial spouse is highly unfair.

More than two-thirds of the states use a method for determining child support called the "income shares" approach.[12] This approach is based on the concept that the children's proportion of total parental income should not be affected by the divorce. A total amount of child support is determined based on the number and age of the children and the combined income of both parents. The amount of child support to be paid by the noncustodial parent is calculated by multiplying his or her share of parental income by the total amount of child support required.

A few states base their guidelines on the Melson formula. The Melson formula is an enhancement of the income shares model. It takes into account the needs of the parents to support themselves. A self-support reserve is taken out of each parent's income prior to the calculation of that share of the children's basic support. The Melson is more complex than the other approaches but, because it incorporates the parent's needs, parents generally perceive it to be the fairest approach.

Although the state child support guidelines take into account the number of children, they also recognize that raising two children is not twice as expensive as raising one. Therefore, the guidelines reduce the support amount per child in larger families to best approximate the true needs.

One major motivation for the creation of child support guidelines was to reduce poverty in single parent households. If this were their only use they might only apply to those with lower incomes. However, the guidelines in most states were designed to apply to most people. For those families with the highest incomes, many states cap the amount of child support required by the guidelines. Generally, such fortunate couples agree that an appropriate amount for child support exceeds the minimums identified by the guidelines. If they do not, the court can still require such higher payments in order to meet the children's pre-divorce standard of living.

In some states, support orders are automatically reviewed every few years to make sure payments are consistent with current income and the support guidelines.[13] The guidelines themselves are also reviewed periodically and such reviews have become quite contentious affairs. In some cases states have made significant changes in state guidelines. When this occurs parents may be allowed to revisit their support orders to take advantage of increases or reductions in the amount they receive or pay.

One of the explicit goals states have when they create child support guidelines is to improve the efficiency of the court system by promoting settlements. Since so many child support arrangements are arrived at outside of court, and some states do not require the arrangements to be reviewed by a court, we advise parents to avoid an arrangement that results in anything less than the guideline amount. Such agreements, even when they include alternate compensation, can open the door to a future lawsuit for failure to pay the guideline amount. Regardless of any agreement you make with your former spouse, the court maintains an interest in your children's well-being until they are independent.

Information about each state's child support guidelines can be found online.

## Identifying Income

When divorcing couples divide their property they, or their lawyers, often search for hidden assets to ensure a fair settlement or judgment. Child support is based on income, which results in a search for all sources of income. Information about the bulk of income for wage earners is found on pay stubs. They reveal the gross income, required deductions for taxes, and discretionary deductions for things like a retirement or medical savings plan. Some people overwithhold their taxes so they can receive a tax refund. This results in an artificial reduction in income that will undoubtedly be noticed during the review of income that will be performed as part of determining child support obligations.

In some states, the court may consider overtime wages in determining child support, if the overtime is a regular part of the employment and the employee can actually expect to regularly earn a certain amount of income from working overtime. In determining whether overtime pay is a regular part of employment, the court may consider such factors as the work history of the employee for the employer, the degree of control the employee has over work conditions, and the nature of the employer's business or industry.

People whose income is highly commission-based or who are self-employed present a special challenge when it comes to agreeing on the amount of income to be used for the calculation of child support. Those on commission may have good years and bad years. Their income for the purposes of child support will generally be an average of their income over several years. Similarly, self-employed people may have irregular income. Sometimes this is due to a decision to invest sweat equity into the business rather than paying themselves. Such a choice may be challenged during negotiations or in court to ensure an appropriate basis for child support.

It has become common for people to change jobs, and even careers, many times throughout their working years. Some of these changes are voluntary, and some are involuntary, such as those due to market changes. While married, parents may choose to make career decisions that would result in a reduction of income and standard of living. After a divorce, this freedom may be limited. A child support payer who reduces his or her income, whether due to anger at their former spouse, a desire to try something new, or any other reason, may find that the court cares little about the motivation.

All state child support guidelines include a mechanism to handle situations in which a payer is not earning at the level he or she could. When a parent is determined to be unemployed or underemployed, a court is authorized to assume income at "earning capacity." The court can base its calculation of earning capacity on factors such as work history, education, skills, and job opportunities. Earning capacity is not limited to wage-earning capacity, but includes moneys available from all sources. This means that an investment that once produced income, but was transferred to a long-term appreciating asset, could be considered when determining income.

---

# When State Guidelines Don't Fit

The child support guidelines have become more of the rule than the exception in determining the amount of support to be paid. However, they are not set in stone, and each state allows variation from the guidelines. Judges must justify any deviation in a written finding. Among the justifications judges may use are:

- The overall financial situation of one spouse
- The net income of the parent after required withholdings.

- The number and needs of other dependents of a parent.
- The physical, mental, and emotional health needs of the child.
- The child's standard of living during the marriage.
- The custody or visitation arrangement, such as summers with noncustodial parent.
- The cost of child care required to allow a parent to work.
- The tax consequences to each party.
- The children's cost of living as a result of moving to a new state.

While many people focus on the simple calculation provided by their state's guidelines, an experienced lawyer will consider the whole picture, and may be able to justify a substantial variance from the guidelines. Upward deviation typically occurs in families of wealth, or in families where the children have unusual needs. Downward deviation typically occurs when either the custodial parent does not require the full guideline amount to meet the child's reasonable needs, or when the noncustodial parent does not have the ability to pay the amount dictated by the guidelines.

# Medical Expenses

Parents are, of course, responsible for the medical expenses of their children. The bulk of these expenses are covered by health insurance in most families. There is no standard approach among states as to how the cost of insurance or the cost of uncovered medical expenses figures into child support orders. Typically, parents will identify the spouse whose plan allows for the addition of the children at the lowest cost, and calculate payment to that spouse for the insurance into their agreement. Additional expenses are typically split based on relative total or discretionary income. If the parents cannot agree on how to cover medical expenses, a judge will decide for them, and the result may not be the lowest cost solution.

# College Expenses

States differ on whether divorced parents must pay for college or trade school. About half the states allow the court to require parents to pay. Several factors may be considered by a judge, including the parents' ability to pay, the child's ability to benefit from the education, the expectations set when the parents were together, the parents' level of education, and the child's age. Courts reason that the child's education should not suffer because of the divorce.

Regardless of the state law, parents can, of course, agree to the payment of college support, and can specify those details in their divorce agreement. Your state may have precedents setting out what terms must be in a college support provision so that it can be enforced by a court. Ideally, the agreement will specify the maximum number of consecutive semesters, the total annual payment (potentially tied to the cost of a benchmark school, such as a major state university), the expenses to be included, the effect of grants, scholarships, and loans on the support, and how any educational savings will be used.

# Child Support vs. Child Custody

In almost all cases, one parent has primary custody of the couple's children. However, when there is real shared physical custody, where the children spend a substantial amount of time with each parent, the payment of child support can be greatly affected. In these cases, the amount of time the child spends with each parent is taken into account, along with their relative incomes. In a situation where custody was shared 50/50 and incomes were equal, there would likely be no child support paid by either party. Where custody and income is unequal, child support payments help balance the financial responsibilities involved in raising the children.

The fact that sharing physical custody can affect child support payments has injected a financial element into custody negotiations. Although it is a stretch, some attorneys will advise clients to increase their share of custody in order to reduce or eliminate child support payments. Aside from the fact that such advice is not based on what is in the children's best interests, it is not financially sound. Child support payments are almost always less than the real costs associated with raising the children. Increasing your share of custody will not reduce your real expenses.

# Accounting for Child Support

The biggest source of friction about child support is the lack of accountability for how the funds are spent. The funds provided for child support must be spent for the benefit of the children. Using the funds for other purposes may result in a court intervention. However, most states do not make any provision to allow the payer to receive an accounting of the funds. As a result of lobbying by fathers' rights groups, a number of states have added such a provision. Regardless, getting an accounting requires a court order, and the courts have generally interpreted the right as a narrow one.

Advocates of requiring accounting of child support spending claim it would improve the rate of compliance with child support orders because noncustodial parents would be more likely to believe that their money was being spent as intended. Opponents argue that there is no evidence that this is the case. They say that allowing payers to request accountings gives too much control to the noncustodial parent, and undermines the custodial parent's decision-making authority.

Payers concerned about this issue may be able to negotiate an accounting of their child-support funds into their divorce agreement. Alternatively, they may specify that they will directly pay certain bills, such as private school, and reduce the monthly support payment accordingly. They must use care, however, to avoid reducing their payment below the level specified by the state guidelines, in order to avoid the potential for a lawsuit due to underpayment of support.

# Modifying Child Support

Child support orders can generally be changed by the agreement of both spouses. Any change would need to be in writing, and must be signed by a judge. If parents cannot agree, the parent wanting to change court ordered child support must persuade the court that there has been a "significant change of circumstance" since the last order, which has resulted in an inability to pay or an inability to live on the ordered support. Changes that may qualify include a substantial decrease in income of either parent, a significant raise for the noncustodial parent, an improvement in the custodial parent's finances due to an inheritance, or a change in the needs of the child.

Support agreements between parents that were not part of a court order may have their own terms and mechanisms for modification. This is one of the many reasons that we recommend that parents consult an attorney before signing an initial agreement; if you are not intimately familiar with your state's child support guidelines, it is unlikely that you will be able to anticipate the issues that will impact your ability to tweak your agreement in later years. We have seen cases in which the support-paying spouse went to court to request a reduction in support amount, and wound up having to pay *more* per month, not less. Judges are pretty much bound by the state-mandated child support guidelines, and you need to be aware of what those guidelines are in your state, before you sign any agreement.

# Child Support and Taxes

Unlike alimony, child support is not considered taxable income and is not tax deductible to the payer. In some cases couples who are considering an amount of child support in excess of the minimum required by the state guidelines may wish to divert some of those funds to alimony. This creates an advantage for the payer in situations where the payer is in a higher tax bracket than the receiver. In exchange for creating such an advantage for the payer, the receiving spouse may be able to negotiate a higher overall payment. However, it's important to keep in mind that the alimony recipient will typically have a higher tax bill. A lawyer or accountant can help determine the net effect of such a switch, taking into account the recipient's current and potential future earnings. Depending on your particular circumstances, the tax implications of child support may or may not have a significant impact on your budget. The bottom line is that each party will need to look rationally at his or her financial situation, and the two of you will have to work out a solution that takes advantage of every option for the overall financial health of this new family arrangement.

## Leaving the Nest

Just as in married families, children must eventually leave the nest and become independent. When exactly child support ends varies from state to state, but is typically between eighteen and twenty-one (when the child becomes a legal adult). Other situations may result in an even earlier termination of support, such as the child taking action to become a legal adult before they reach the standard age, entrance into the military, work at a full-time job, marriage, or death.

Families with multiple children to support will want to ensure that their agreement recognizes that the children (unless they are twins) will reach adulthood at different times. The agreement can scale back support as each child's needs are satisfied. The state guidelines are a good source of reference for negotiating the degree to which support should change as the number of children to be supported changes.

## Ensuring Child Support is Paid

Historically, child support payments have not been taken seriously, and most commonly were not paid or not paid in full. Strong efforts have been made over the last two decades to improve the situation. The situation has improved, but there are still many families living in poverty as a result of unpaid child support.

The most common way of ensuring that child support is paid is through a wage deduction order. This order requires an employer to send a portion of the obligor-parent's wages to a state agency. That agency then forwards the funds to the custodial parent.

Current law makes wage deductions the standard for all child support orders. The wage deduction can be waived by the court or by agreement of the parties. Even with a waiver, if payments become thirty days overdue, wage deductions must begin. Employers must support the system by notifying the state when employees are hired or terminated.

One downside of wage deductions is that they are not effective against obligors who are self-employed. This is one reason why other tools exist to collect support. The state can intercept federal and state tax refunds to pay past due child support obligations. Almost every state has made it impossible for nonpayers to receive driver, professional, sporting, and other licenses. Additionally, the state can place liens on the obligor's property, such as real estate and automobiles. The court may also hold an obligor in contempt of court as a result of ignoring the court's order. A finding of contempt can result in a fine, a jail term, or both.

The federal government has mandated that states create a child support enforcement agency, which can assist with collecting unpaid child support. Additionally, attorneys can assist with child support collection. Unlike in most family law issues, an attorney may be compensated for work done in collecting past due child support through a contingency agreement. This means the lawyer retains a percentage (typically one-third) of any funds collected. The client pays nothing for the lawyer's time if the collection effort is unsuccessful. Private debt collection firms can also work to collect unpaid support and also will do so on a contingency basis.

# Plan for the Long Term and the Unexpected

As in most negotiations it is important to not limit your consideration to the present but to comprehensively consider what might happen in the future. People are shocked when child support changes. They think of the money as something that will continue forever unchanged. However, if the payer loses a job, becomes disabled, or dies, the child support will likely be reduced or stopped. In some states (North Carolina is one) the child support agreement can be a contract between the spouses rather than a court order. If the contract does not allow for modification without the agreement of both parties, a spouse whose income drops (and who subsequently fails to make support payments) could have assets seized.

Disability and death can be addressed by the purchase of disability and life insurance policies for the benefit of the children. Since both spouses will usually be contributing to the children's care, either in cash or in time, it is advisable to insure both parties. Your agreement or court order may state that you must present proof of insurance to your spouse annually.

We have seen clients lose a job, but remain optimistic about regaining the previous income level quickly. When the new job opportunities don't materialize, it's easy to suddenly fall behind on support payments and wind up in court asking for a modification to court-ordered child support. It's important to know that federal law forbids a judge form making changes retroactively. Any accumulated child support amounts due must be paid. People who experience such an unexpected change in circumstance must act quickly by talking to an attorney about their options for modifying their support.

In our experience, noncustodial parents often wish to continue the vision they had for their children when things were going well in their marriage. They may have dreamed of sending the children to a special baseball camp or supporting an interest in music. These are admirable wishes that we wholeheartedly support. However, when negotiating child support we advise our clients to be careful about obligating themselves to pay more than the guidelines indicate. There is nothing that prevents a parent from paying more than the agreed-upon amount if the money is available, or from picking up the tab for specific items. Our concern arises from the possibility that an individual with the means to provide more at one time may not always be in the same financial situation.

Although there are many hard-to-predict circumstances that may arise while raising your children, inflation is not one of them. We all know that the cost of living will rise over time. A child support agreement can take inflation into account by providing for annual increases based on the consumer price index as published by the Department of Labor. The main sticking point when adding such a provision is the legitimate concern that a payer's income may not rise as rapidly as inflation. To address this fear, the agreement can specify that the increase will be capped so it does not exceed any increase in the parent's income.

## Negotiating Child Support

As in all aspects of divorce, negotiating a settlement for child support is far preferable to having one imposed by the court. The unique aspects and desires of your family can be taken into account during negotiations. In court, long-lasting decisions are made quickly by someone who knows very little about your family. Issues such as college, medical expenses, and the way in which the child support will vary as your lives change can be carefully thought through and spelled out when negotiation succeeds.

There are a few pitfalls we want to help you avoid as you attempt to negotiate child support with your spouse, either directly or with the help of an intermediary. It is important that the custodial parent avoid becoming the sole advocate for the children in the negotiations. This arrangement creates short and long-term problems. A custodial parent demanding more funds is often mistaken for a person fighting for more personal funds. Non-custodial parents can feel that increases in child support are effectively additional alimony. Divorced parents need to each take responsibility for caring for children's financial needs. They must make the economic decisions about the children jointly. This requires both parents to consider what the kids need, which needs have priority, and which can be funded.

The frequent inability to fund all needs is another area where couples can stumble as one parent may insist that the children's lives not be affected by the parents' divorce. To the extent possible, that's great, but for most couples the additional expenses of maintaining two households make some cutting necessary. When this occurs it may be necessary for parents to jointly communicate with their children about what has happened (such as the inability to maintain a club membership or attend summer camp) so blame isn't placed on one parent alone. Changes in one area of a budget (such as the elimination of camp) can result in new costs (additional child care). Each parent must work to anticipate the effects of budget changes and ensure that new needs are met.

The most important tip we find ourselves giving to divorcing couples is to try and separate their feelings about their spouse (and the breakup) from their relationship with their children. If you can step back from the emotional turmoil that surrounds a divorce, and see the bigger picture of how you will interact with your kids over the next twenty or thirty years, you may be able to think impartially about child support in terms of a parenting issue, rather than a divorce issue. We find, unfortunately, that some people are unable to gain this perspective, and instead use child support negotiations as a forum in which to voice issues that have nothing to do with the children, thereby prolonging a marital relationship that needs to be over. Remember that you will be a co-parent with this person long after you are no longer married; you need to learn how to communicate calmly and neutrally, for the sake of your children. Child support is not about you; it's about your kids.

# Notes

[12] "Guideline Models by State," *Washington State Department of Social and Health Services.*
http://www.dshs.wa.gov/pdf/esa/dcs/guidelinemodels.pdf.

[13] "Setting Guidelines for Child Support," *American Bar Association.*
http://www.americanbar.org/groups/public_education/resources/law_issues_for_consumers/childsupport_guidelines.html.

# Part Three:
# The Best Way to
# Complete Your Divorce

# Achieving Your Best Outcome

Now that you have worked through the issues of property, alimony, custody, and child support, the last step you need to take to finish this process is to actually finalize your divorce. Ironically, the absolute divorce is generally the easiest and simplest element of a divorce—it is, basically, the official and public statement that the two of you no longer wish to be married. From a legal perspective, it is important that you take this final step; your marital status matters in the world (legally, financially, etc.), and the only way to be "officially" divorced is to sign the papers. We do occasionally see clients who, for various and complicated reasons, have great difficulty finishing the process, and years later are still unable to find closure. We urge you: finalize the divorce, sign the papers, and get on with your life. The divorce itself is really just a formality—do it, and move on.

It is necessary, at this point, to revisit the Spectrum of Control, which we first mentioned back in "An Overview of Divorce." Now that you have thought through the multitude of issues surrounding the dissolution of your marriage, you need to make a decision regarding the fundamental emotional tenor of your divorce. Basically, all divorcing couples exercise a measure of control over their situation that ranges somewhere between kitchen-table negotiations, with no outside involvement, and a court-ordered resolution that is determined and mandated by a judge. Very few of our clients go to the extreme poles; most cases get settled somewhere in the middle, by one of three means—collaboration, mediation, or lawyer-led settlement. You need to decide how much control you want to have over this major life change. As you are thinking about where *you* fall along the Spectrum of Control, keep in mind the following points:

First, the more you know, the better off you are and the more likely it is that you will achieve a better divorce outcome. Knowledge is power-- that's the long and short of it.

Second, the more time you spend planning for your future, making your own decisions and mapping out the course that will best work for you, the more likely it will be that the results of the separation and divorce will feel satisfying to you. If you take responsibility for your life now, you will feel less helpless during separation and divorce, even in the midst of strong negative feelings. If you totally "hand off" your divorce to someone else, either your spouse or your own attorney, without directly participating in the process, it is more likely you'll feel like you don't know what is going on. In many senses, that will probably be true. Losing control of your life in this way will leave you worse off than you can possibly imagine. In all likelihood, you will be worse off both emotionally and financially than you will be if you participate actively in resolving the issues arising from your separation.

Third, you need to try to view the resolution of matrimonial legal issues as a business transaction. Dividing property, deciding on residential arrangements for children, arranging for payments of child support and alimony can all be see as business arrangements. You may have lots of feelings over one or more of these issues, but don't let your feelings get tangled up with your business sense. Remember, then, to keep the settlement of your legal issues unencumbered, to the fullest extent possible, from all the petty emotional struggles that will only drag out the process and drag you down as well. These three basic principles will take you a long way in mapping out your own divorce with the least possible pain and expense.

Finally, what are you going to learn from this process? Admittedly, the unraveling of a marriage is not generally seen as a positive event, but as we keep pointing out, if you can see it as a challenge to grow and stretch yourself, you may find that when all is said and done, you will be a stronger, better person. Major life changes always present opportunities for personal growth—perhaps you can learn to be a better communicator, a stronger negotiator, or a more patient parent. There are people in the world who spend their lives learning and changing and growing, and there are others who stagnate. A divorce presents a fairly unique opportunity for radical growth at a stage in life when it's easy to stagnate—try to take advantage of the potential for growth.

## Settlement: The Most Attractive Option

The vast majority of divorce cases will be *settled,* meaning that the parties will reach some sort of agreement without litigation, or the intervention of a judge. Settlement is preferable in almost every case for any number of reasons. In almost all cases, resolution through settlement is less costly, less prolonged and less emotionally draining than litigation. The emotional strain of court proceedings is felt, moreover, by each spouse (regardless of who initiated the litigation) and also by the children, by other family members, and by friends and work associates who interact with the litigating spouses. Divorce—even without litigation—is already a major emotional stress on any family. The change in family living arrangements alone causes temporary adjustment problems for the most sturdy of individuals. Added to such changes is all the uncertainty involved in reallocating family financial resources that once went to one intact family unit and must now stretch to meet the needs of two households.

It is, then, little wonder that many families feel crushed by the extra emotional wear and tear of having to deal with court papers, including the burdensome discovery process of sharing written documents and answering written or oral questions, the selection and interviews of potential witnesses, and all the anxiety of formal court proceedings. Litigation is enough of a strain when it doesn't feel like the whole web of one's life is falling apart all at once. When one's concept of who one is and what the future will hold is being altered by separation and divorce, sometimes radically altered, then litigation is almost more than some people can bear.

Another disadvantage to litigation is that the judge, and not either of the contestants, dictates the result. Once your case is litigated, you lose control over the process even when you think you (and your attorney) are influencing the judge. The outcome of litigation is, moreover, never a real victory for either side. Each side loses from having had to go through adversary proceedings. It's not only parents who suffer from courtroom proceedings. The children will be traumatized as well, whether or not they ever set foot in the courthouse.

Just as important as minimizing emotional and financial devastation at a time of major personal crisis, settlement can be custom-tailored to a family's interests and needs in a way that may not occur in the bureaucratic judicial system. That system cannot know your personal priorities and your family's special traditions the same way you and your spouse know those priorities and traditions. The judicial system is, on the whole, conservative in fashioning remedies. The system will not provide the kind of creative solutions that you and your spouse might create on your own, provided you both have the stamina necessary for negotiation and the capacity to be flexible. For all these reasons, you want to go to court only as a last resort, when nothing else looks like it will work.

Regardless of whether spouses can settle or they are forced to litigate, the independent nature of custody, support and property issues in some states can drag out the ultimate resolution of all issues arising from separation. For example, in North Carolina, custody can and might be resolved—by private agreement or in court—long before any other topics have been dealt with, or, property might be divided long before there are any agreements with respect to custody or support. You will certainly want to consider, during the negotiation process, whether it makes sense to try to deal with all issues simultaneously, rather than one at a time. In terms of peace of mind, closure and expense, it usually makes the most sense to settle everything at once and as expeditiously as possible under your individual circumstances.

It is, of course, also often tactically advantageous to settle as many issues as possible all at once. A prime advantage of such a settlement technique is that either husband or wife has the opportunity to "trade" or compromise on items in one subject area (such as custody) for something the other spouse wants more in another area (such as property). If, by comparison, all five topics are dealt with at separate times, as North Carolina law permits, "trading" across subject areas is going to be much more limited.

One piece of advice that helps many of our clients is the idea of focusing most of your attention on the single issue that is most important to you (rather than allowing yourself to get sidetracked on issues that have only passing or minor emotional significance), and then to be prepared to make concessions on the matter that counts most to your spouse. If, however, you can see, ahead of time, that your most important issue is also your spouse's most important issue, and the two of you are in opposite camps over that issue, negotiating may be a waste of time. But on the other hand, if you have figured out what your spouse most wants, and you can find a way to make that happen, then you may have some leverage in getting what *you* most want.

Focusing on your single most important priority and your spouse's highest priority are extremely important tactics that are all too often overlooked in negotiations. Let's say you have two teenagers, both of whom hope and plan to go to college. You and your spouse quickly drew up and signed a separation agreement and property settlement addressing only property and custody. Both children will reside with you. All the marital property, including the IRAs in your spouses's name, has been equally divided between you and your partner in the written agreement.

You entered into the written agreement, drafted without a lawyer, at a time that both of you foresaw that you would have to ask a judge to decide the issue of child support because the two of you had sharp disagreements over that. You drafted the agreement yourselves, covering only custody and property, because you and your spouse perceived both of those areas to be simple enough to do on your own. There was simply no contest over custody. You yourself felt especially secure about the property issues, too, because you have always managed the family finances. You were certain that you were not overlooking any marital assets when you tallied everything up. You also believed that all assets had been fairly valued and divided. You and your spouse researched sample language for your written agreement in several legal texts; both of you understood your contract would be a binding agreement, and you are both confident that there are no major omissions or mistakes in the drafting you did. Thus, you are not really concerned about the future implementation of the custody and property agreement that the two of you have finalized.

You left child support out of your settlement discussions and the written agreement, however, based on your perception of your children's financial needs and based on a concern that you might not have been able to draft an "air-tight" document concerning support. You believed the children would be entitled to receive monthly support above the Child Support Guidelines, which your spouse would not agree to. You were both prepared, in the heat of angry conversations, to litigate the issue. You and your spouse never discussed the children's future college expenses, as the issue of child support was something the two of you did not discuss in any detail once it became clear that you were not going to be able to agree.

Now you have realized that getting your partner to agree to contribute to the children's college education is much more important to you than having half of their IRAs, and contribution to college education is also now far more important to you than asking a judge to award monthly child support above the Guideline amount, which the judge might refuse to do anyway. You have also now been informed, correctly, that a North Carolina judge lacks the authority to order a parent to pay for college expenses unless the judge is merely enforcing a prior contract entered into between two married people. You did not know that earlier, just as you did not recognize earlier that college was a big deal for you.

At this point, you will be able to get your spouse to agree to contribute to college costs, if at all, only by reopening the negotiations that had previously resulted in a written agreement. Your spouse may be interested enough in retaining all of their IRAs or in getting some other item of property, that they would consent to sign a new agreement that obligates contributions toward college. Or, it could be that your spouse has now gotten used to the idea that their IRAs are divided with you, according to what both of you deemed to be fair, as well as the idea of just letting a judge decide about monthly child support. In other words, your spouse may no longer be interested in further negotiations with you.

The opportunity you once had for a more comprehensive settlement may be lost. Worse, you may be left with a bargain not as good as the one you might have struck with your spouse initially. After enduring the stress (and possible expense, if lawyers were involved) of strenuous negotiations, parties may understandably be very reluctant to return to the bargaining table.

Therefore, you want to know—from the start—exactly where you want to go with the negotiations. You also want to become more informed about some of the skills needed for successful negotiations. You can pick up tips about negotiating from a number of excellent books. A good place to start is with *Getting to Yes: Negotiating Agreements Without Giving In* by Fisher and Ury. The chapters in that book summarize some important points to keep in mind at all times: Don't bargain over positions. Separate the people from the problem. Focus on interests, not positions. Invent options for mutual gain. Insist on using objective criteria. Know what to do if the other side is more powerful, or won't play, or is using dirty tricks.

Negotiating in the face of the breakup of a marriage is a daunting task. The conflict with your spouse can get destructive. Negotiations may get seriously out of control. One party may commit too early to something that he or she can't or won't do. Separation distress can be greatly augmented if settlement discussions aren't mutual efforts to work out practical solutions that make sense for both partners and the children. Most couples cannot go it alone (remember the kitchen-table end of the Spectrum of Control?), but need to rely on lawyers or other professionals to smooth the way.

Before we discuss the various kinds of third-party help available to assist with negotiations, we'd like to give a few tidbits of advice to those of you who *are* planning to draw up an agreement at the kitchen table: It is, of course, extremely difficult for each spouse not to become embroiled in the issues that led to marital dissolution, whether outside help is enlisted for the negotiations or not. Your very best preparation for negotiations is to get your emotions under control and to inform yourself, as fully as possible, about: (1) what you most need and want, (2) what your spouse most wants, (3) what the law says each of you is entitled to, and (4) what your family income and expenses are now and what they will be post-separation. Don't try to negotiate without getting a handle on this information, whether you are negotiating on your own behalf or you are using someone to negotiate for you. Don't try to continue negotiations at a juncture at which one, or both, of you has lost objectivity.

Here are some tactics and attitudes to adopt, if you do decide to try one-on-one negotiations with your spouse. Negotiate in a neutral place where you feel safe, at a preplanned time. Break off negotiations immediately if things heat up unconstructively. A good starting point for settlement discussions is for you and your spouse to recognize, and enumerate, all the areas on which you agree.

Then find out more about all the things about which you can't agree. Try to hear what your spouse has to say, without arguing the points. Try to get your spouse to hear what you have to say, without raising your voice. Be careful not to fence yourself in by indicating some dollar amount that you are offering, or that you are willing to accept. If you offer a dollar amount that you later realize was too high, your spouse's expectations have been set at the higher amount. If you said you'd take an amount that you subsequently discover is too little to meet your expenses, you will have a devil of a time convincing your spouse to increase the amount. Think about the items of property you are receiving when you and your spouse make guesses about their value—the lower the values on the items you will be receiving, and the higher the value of your spouse's items, the more items you will get in a 50 percent division.

Address all the issues, not just some of the issues; look at the facts, not what you or your spouse imagine to be the facts; see if the two of you can create solutions rather than new areas for conflict. At impasses, talk together about what the likely outcome would be if you have to go to court. In order to make these predictions, you both need to know the basic materials presented in this book. You also need to look for points on which to leverage your requests. Such points include secrets that your spouse doesn't want to make public, or your spouse's sense of duty or your spouse's pride in being known to do the right thing.

Remember, statistics predict that you will settle the issues that may seem to be impossible to settle. But if you can't settle under your own power, don't wear yourself out trying. Just move on to the next step—get help from an attorney or another professional. If that person picks up the negotiations, the discussions may go on for some time. There may be telephone calls, letters, demands/counteroffers, proposed draft agreements, face-to-face meetings, and delays. Still, you will most likely settle eventually.

# Collaborative Divorce

The next stop along the Spectrum of Control, if kitchen-table negotiations clearly aren't going to work, is collaborative divorce.

## Collaborative Divorce - A No-Court, Solutions-Based Approach

How can you divide twelve oranges in half and still give both parties twelve oranges? Depending on the part of the orange each wants (the zest or the meat), the division can be fast, simple, and mutually gratifying—as long as both parties understand what is valuable to the other. In a nutshell, or perhaps one should say "under the peel," this is the appeal of collaborative divorce law in settling divorce cases.

Collaborative divorce is a new way for a divorcing couple to work as a team with trained professionals to resolve disputes respectfully, without going to court. In a collaborative divorce, each spouse has the support, protection and guidance of his or her own lawyer. Often, other professionals such as child specialists, financial specialists and divorce coaches will be brought in to advise on matters in their areas of expertise. Lawyers practicing collaborative divorce have competed extensive training in nonadversarial conflict resolution strategies, and clients commit to seeing the process through, or starting over with new lawyers (and new bills!) if negotiations break down.

The vast majority of all divorce cases are settled outside of court anyway, so it stands to reason that nationwide, collaborative divorce law is attracting considerable attention as a proactive and humane settlement option. And so it should! Studies show that when carried out as agreed

205

upon by divorcing individuals and their attorneys, the collaborative process settles issues faster than other forms of negotiation, and greatly reduces the emotional trauma families experience in the throes of a divorce, especially the children. It also significantly lowers the expenses incurred by divorcing couples, protecting families from unnecessary resource depletion at a time when funds are needed to establish two households.

Collaborative Divorce is not a dispute resolution option in the same sense as mediation or arbitration. Rather, collaborative divorce is a set of voluntary ground rules entered into by divorcing couples and their attorneys. It is a client-centered, interest-based negotiation model for resolving disputes. While the details vary from practitioner to practitioner, the central idea is that the parties retain attorneys who agree in advance not to take the case to trial, and who agree to full disclosure of information. You and your attorneys forswear litigation and, in the end, if your case cannot be settled and you decide to litigate, you both have to hire new attorneys, as outlined by collaborative divorce rules.

The collaborative divorce model was developed in the early 1990s by a practicing family law attorney who saw the need for a kinder, gentler alternative to the adversarial system. He developed a training program and began teaching lawyers all over the country how to both practice and replicate his system. At the same time, collaborative resource organizations sprang up, enabling practitioners to both rely on and, to a certain extent, hold each other accountable. Most states now have networks of collaborative lawyers who have been trained in the system, and have met the standards of practice laid out in the original materials.

If you are the kind of couple that is determined to hire lawyers only if you can't work it out and things gets really ugly, then collaborative divorce may very well be for you. This process allows you all the benefits of legal counsel without the threat of a court battle, or some of the other negative aspects of involving combatant lawyers in your divorce process. Engaging in the collaborative process may also reduce some of the stress and tension in your personal life, as you are going through the process of divorce and trying to establish the groundwork for a new beginning.

Collaborative divorce lawyers help you make knowledgeable decisions about financial issues. For example, they advise you about the hidden pitfalls of the tax code and the intricate rules imposed by the US Department of Labor and Internal Revenue Service governing retirement plans. They make sure you don't make document drafting mistakes that cost both parties in ways they didn't expect. Collaborative Divorce lawyers make sure you understand the law, your rights, your obligations, and the legal effects of your decisions. They also help make the process of separating your assets more peaceful, as they focus on positive communication methods and making requests versus demands from the other party. There is a strong focus on respect throughout this process, and that is one of the many things that make it a potentially great option. This approach is much less difficult for everyone and helps build a rapport between the two sides instead of potential bitterness. Collaborative divorce gives you all of the benefits of good legal representation without the potential negative factors involved with other options, such as arbitration or litigation.

The Collaborative Divorce process requires that both your lawyer and your spouse's lawyer be trained in collaborative divorce. Lawyers must undergo specialized instruction to develop collaborative negotiation skills. The governing body that teaches the collaborative process is the International Academy of Collaborative Professionals; this group also maintains a current list of practitioners. Use that list to have a conversation with your spouse, and agree to each meet with a lawyer from the list. There are all kinds of lawyers on the list, and you should be able to find someone with the knowledge, experience, personal characteristics, and personality you are seeking.

Collaborative lawyers are trained and skilled in collaborative law to create an open environment that encourages the peaceful resolution of issues. Like arbitration, collaborative law requires all parties to sign a document. This is called a Collaborative Law Agreement and states that the parties commit: 1) to resolve the issues outside of court, 2) to honestly communicate all relevant facts and financial matters, and 3) to disqualify their attorneys from further representation if the matter is not resolved collaboratively. The first and third statements above can easily be managed. However, it is important for couples to understand up front that each is entrusting his/her soon-to-be former spouse to be honest in the negotiations. Unfortunately, the attorneys have a limited capacity to ensure this honesty. You certainly want to feel confident that your spouse will commit to and follow through with complete honesty and openness, just as you must also commit to do.

As a first step, both the divorcing couple and their attorneys will sign a pledge to participate in the collaborative law process. This will occur before any negotiation begins. The pledge details several principles and guidelines that you all must agree to comply with in order to continue on the path to collaborative divorce.

There are typically about ten sections in the pledge covering a variety of issues. The first section generally outlines some goals to which both parties must agree, such as the idea that a "nonadversarial process" is best to use when resolving conflict, and that there will be a focus on the future well-being of the parties and their families by maintaining an atmosphere of honesty, cooperation, integrity, and professionalism.

The second section of the pledge usually outlines that both parties must agree to no court intervention, as well as to give full and honest disclosure of all information, regardless of whether it's requested or not. Agreeing to participate in mediated settlement conferences, where you will not only express your own needs and desires, but will also hear and recognize the needs and desires of the other party, is also outlined here.

Section III of the pledge acknowledges that any third parties, such as accountants, therapists, or appraisers that are brought in to resolve any issues that may arise will be retained jointly and directed to work in a cooperative effort to resolve the issues.

When it comes to children, while going through the collaborative law process, parents agree to insulate them from involvement in the dispute and not to seek a custody evaluation unless agreed to by both parties. The goal is to resolve any parenting issues in the most amicable manner possible and in the best interests of the children. Section IV of the pledge outlines these goals regarding children.

Section V outlines some of the limitations of the collaborative process. For example, it is a voluntary process, and there is, of course, no guarantee that it will be successful in resolving the case. Although this process can promote healing and growth, it will not necessarily resolve certain feelings and concerns that led to the current conflict.

"Integrity and Good Faith" is the title of the sixth section, and it outlines the idea of "working to maintain a high standard of integrity" and "specifically to not take advantage of the other parties' mistakes or miscalculations, but rather to disclose them and seek to have them corrected." Acting in good faith and protecting both parties' integrity is one of the key underlying goals of the collaborative process and is absolutely necessary in order for it to be successful.

If either attorney feels that his or her client has "intentionally withheld or misrepresented" information in a way that goes against the principles of the collaborative process (rightly or wrongly), he or she may withdraw from the case. Both parties must agree to this, and in Section VII, the provisions of what may be perceived as "withheld or misrepresented information" are outlined.

Section VIII reiterates the idea that both attorneys can never represent their clients in court. If a resolution is not reached through the collaborative process and the parties decide to take the issues to court, they must hire new counsel.

If either party decides that the collaborative process is "no longer appropriate," then the process may be terminated by written notice to the attorneys. Section IX explains this and also states that the process may be terminated if either party files an action or motion in court.

The last section is the actual pledge, which states, "We, the undersigned, pledge to comply with and to promote the spirit and written word of this document." By signing this pledge, the divorcing couple promises, "In an atmosphere of honesty, cooperation, integrity, and professionalism, we will focus on the future well-being of the parties and their families in reaching a settlement."

For many couples, collaborative divorce is a way to avoid litigation and come out of a divorce cooperating on child issues and finishing financial issues in a way that the parties were never able to do during the marriage. People learn new skills to cooperate and communicate. It not only ends the marriage in a positive way, it prepares folks to move forward with their lives and make new relationships work rather than falling back into old patterns. And if there are children involved, the collaborative process lays the groundwork for a more constructive relationship between the divorced parents as the children grow up. Collaborative divorce can help some people see divorce as a learning experience, rather than a total catastrophe.

Like mediation and arbitration, collaborative law attempts to maintain a civil relationship throughout the negotiations process, as well as after an agreement is reached. Other experts are brought into the collaborative process as needed, but only as neutrals jointly retained by both parties. If either you or your spouse becomes uncomfortable in addressing a particular issue, a mediator may be consulted to help with the collaborative process. If the mediator fails to bring closure, or if you or your spouse decides not to attempt mediation, you both must hire new counsel and deal with the unresolved issues in either arbitration or litigation.

Though the negotiations of collaborative divorce often help divorcing couples put their lives back in order, the process is not appropriate for all situations. Couples entering into a collaborative process should feel confident that both parties will be honest and forthcoming throughout the negotiation process.

And if everything works out as planned, both husband and wife take home twelve oranges. What a positive way to begin again in life!

# Mediation

Mediation is the most common dispute resolution option; however, it is often misunderstood. Mediation allows you and your spouse to reach a fair settlement with the help of a third, neutral party called a mediator. Mediators, who can be lawyers, mental health professionals, clergy, or other professionals trained in alternative dispute resolution techniques, help you and your spouse identify and resolve issues. Basically, mediation is similar to sitting down to negotiate with the help of a referee.

The most important thing to understand is that mediators *cannot* give either of you legal advice. They are not a substitute for having your own lawyer. This is one important distinction between mediation and collaborative divorce: collaboration is (generally) an all-inclusive package, while mediation is more like one step (albeit an important one) in the process. You will almost certainly still need to hire an attorney. The mediator's role is to help you and your spouse communicate and reach agreement while your lawyer's role is to make sure your legal rights are protected.

Mediation is confidential, allows you and your spouse to make the decisions, and is less expensive than filing a lawsuit and going to court. The goal is to be able to reach a positive agreement that is more customized than the one you might receive from a judge.

In mediation, you are responsible for your attorney's fees, as well as half of the mediator's fees. In certain states, mediation is required by the court after a lawsuit has been filed; for example, North Carolina requires couples to attend mediation before a child custody trial and equitable distribution trial.

# Disadvantages of Mediation

There are, of course, many advantages to a mediated divorce, the most obvious of which is the diffusion of the negativity that can surround negotiations. A skilled mediator will ratchet down the hostility, enabling both parties to move on with their lives in a positive way. The goal of mediation is to achieve a rapid, low-cost, and reasonable agreement between spouses, and it *sometimes* works. But we have some significant concerns about the way mediation is marketed and practiced at this point in time.

One significant distinction between mediation and collaboration is the amount of training and accountability involved. The vast majority of states do not regulate mediators in any way; there is no required training, no peer-to-peer oversight, and no way to monitor outcomes. Anyone can call him or herself a mediator and hang out a shingle; there is no clear, consistent definition of the term. As a result, there can be dramatic differences between practitioners. There are mediators out there who are well-trained in negotiation skills, well-versed in legal issues, and well-equipped to handle challenging conflicts. But by the same token, there are also mediators out there who are simply not able to give the guidance that most couples need.

One important skill that a trained, experienced mediator brings to the table is the ability to recognize situations in which mediation is NOT appropriate. For instance, an abusive person will manipulate the mediation process to take advantage of or control his or her spouse. We feel very strongly that any hint or history of domestic violence in a relationship automatically means that mediation is not a safe option for that divorcing couple. A good mediator will be able to identify a power imbalance in a relationship and recommend that the parties need to hire attorneys, so that the safety and best interests of the disadvantaged spouse can be protected. Unfortunately, not all mediators have the skills or training necessary to recognize cases that really need legal supervision.

Another disadvantage of using mediation *instead of* the legal system is our concern that some couples, and some mediators, don't have all the information they need to be able to draft comprehensive documents and agreements that account for wide-ranging possibilities. If you don't understand the child support guidelines, you can find yourself in real trouble if your budget suddenly changes and no mechanism for adjusting the payments was built into the agreement. Similarly, if a spouse doesn't understand that the 401K plan is marital property and doesn't stand up for his or her share, that person could lose a significant amount of money. Mediating without a thorough understanding of the big picture and the variety of possible outcomes can be expensive, if not downright dangerous.

Our final observation about mediation is simply that the more people you bring into a process, the more likely it is that mistakes will be made. The best mediators will recommend that both parties hire their own attorneys to physically write up any agreements that are reached during mediation. Unfortunately, this transfer of information from mediator to attorneys opens up multiple cracks in the process, through which important bits can disappear. If one attorney makes three changes to the agreement, and the other only makes two, those changes are not necessarily communicated to all the relevant parties. We have found that entire sections of documents have gotten lost in the paper shuffle between clients, mediator, and attorneys. We find that it's safer for everyone if all the paperwork is done consistently, with a clear, orderly paper trail.

You will find mediators who provide exactly the opposite advice that we are offering you here; some mediators view lawyers as a dark force that almost inevitably creates conflict in a divorce that might have otherwise been resolved amicably. As we wrote above, we agree that some lawyers are overly adversarial and can run up costs unnecessarily. However, our view on this is that a mediator is not a replacement for a lawyer. We wrote earlier about the types of situations in which people should use lawyers in their divorce. If you found that you are in one of these situations we strongly believe you should get legal advice. You may choose some sort of unbundled service rather than a full representation approach, if you prefer, but your risk of something going wrong without legal help is just too high to not at least get input from a lawyer. Recognizing the potential for lawyers to add conflict helps you in choosing a lawyer who is cautious about going down this road and helps you see when it might be happening. With this awareness we believe that the concerns raised by some mediators about the use of lawyers can be overcome.

# Lawyer-Led Negotiation

The question of whether you need an attorney to handle your divorce is one that was not commonly asked a couple of decades ago. But times have changed, and today it is not uncommon for people to get divorced without any assistance from an attorney. Others are using attorneys in new ways, as the availability of alternative and complementary services increases. Law firms are restructuring in order to meet client needs, and many offer one-stop shopping, including financial planning, counseling, and career coaching. And the popular culture model of a *War of the Roses* type of court battle has gone by the wayside. Most attorneys, and their clients, now realize that out-of-court settlement, negotiated by the respective lawyers, is an easier, healthier, and more advantageous way to dissolve a marriage.

There are many reasons to keep attorneys involved in the divorce process; it is, after all, the dissolution of a legal contract, and a change in legal status. Obviously, a competent, experienced attorney understands terminology, procedure, the court system, and the legal code in ways that no lay person can. An attorney who specializes in divorce, moreover, likely has years of experience that can lend wisdom and insight to your specific case, improving your outcome and your overall satisfaction with your divorce.

At the same time, however, there can be disadvantages to involving attorneys in your divorce. Have you ever received an email from someone that rubbed you the wrong way, and then later talked to the person face-to-face about it and learned that they truly did not intend it to mean what you thought? It is common for people who are communicating without the benefit of face-to-face interaction to misinterpret parts of the communication. Of course the chance of this increases when people are going through a divorce and have had their trust eroded. You need to keep this in mind as you negotiate using a process that reduces or eliminates your direct interactions with your spouse.

Likewise, you need to be prepared for the possibility that negotiations can quickly turn adversarial. When lawyers are involved in the divorce process, the potential for going to court is always on the table. Lawyers frequently rely on their expectation of what a judge would do if the case went to court to fortify their bargaining position. That is, if you are likely to pay your spouse some amount of spousal support, your spouse's attorney is likely to use his or her experience with similar cases to determine whether this is a reasonable deal for your ex. If your ex's attorney thinks your current offer is too low, he or she is likely to threaten taking the case to a judge. Sometimes this is simply a tactic, but you need to discipline yourself to stay calm throughout the negotiation process, and let your attorney know what your absolute limits really are.

Even if you do hire an attorney, chances are you will ultimately wind up settling the issues (whatever those are in your specific case) in out-of-court negotiations. The vast majority of attorneys recognize that taking a case to trial is (usually) unnecessarily adversarial, time-consuming, and expensive, for everyone involved. As a result, your attorney will most likely work pretty hard to help you and your spouse work out the details and arrangements of your divorce without going to court.

Negotiations begin as soon as you hire a lawyer. You should make your priorities clear in your first meeting with legal counsel. He or she will then likely be in contact with your spouse's attorney, and the two will begin the process of give-and-take, consulting with you, drafting and re-drafting documents, until there is an agreement that everyone can be happy with. In many cases, a face-to-face settlement conference can expedite matters; the four of you (two attorneys, two clients) get together in a conference room and just stay there until you've hashed out the details.

Ultimately, the goal is for you to walk away from your marriage with the least amount of unnecessary upset possible. In our experience, the client's satisfaction with his or her divorce is a direct reflection of how much control he or she had over the process. This almost invariably means that some kind of out-of-court settlement is preferable to a trial.

# Arbitration

Arbitration is yet another alternative dispute resolution option that involves a third party called an arbitrator. Basically, arbitration is a private trial in which the parties have hired their own "judge," and have agreed to abide by that person's ruling. Arbitrators, unlike mediators, are professionals trained to hear testimony, take evidence, and issue actual decisions for the couple. These experts are often attorneys and/or retired judges.

When a couple decides to arbitrate their case, all parties involved must initially sign an arbitration agreement. This document gives the arbitrator decision-making authority, narrows the issues to be arbitrated (frequently issues that weren't resolved through mediation) and defines whether the arbitrated award will be binding and thus become a court order.

As in mediation, you and your spouse usually both hire attorneys to help with the arbitration process so that you are both advised and represented by an experienced divorce lawyer. During arbitration there is an actual "hearing," similar to a court hearing, but in a less formal setting. There are opening statements, presentation of the evidence, cross-examination, and closing arguments. The significant advantage of arbitration is that the "hearing" part of the process can go much faster than it might in front of a judge, who has to deal with many cases at once in a busy courtroom. In arbitration, you have your arbitrator's undivided attention, and he or she can move through the issues much more quickly. This speed factor can be both a financial and emotional relief.

As is the case in a court trial, you have little control over the outcome. Arbitration is not always confidential depending on what your signed arbitration agreement states. This option also tends to be more expensive than mediation because you and your spouse not only have to pay for an arbitrator and each of your attorney fees, but, depending on the complexity, the "trial" preparation is often as extensive and time-consuming as preparing for an actual trial. On the whole, though, arbitration can be a useful alternative for a couple who find themselves unable to settle one or more of their disputed issues.

# Litigation

In our experience, most clients, even those who initially come into our office determined to wreak havoc in the ex's life, ultimately settle down and come to recognize that settling the case is far preferable to a living through a trial. But some clients have to take a long, hard look at themselves and their situation before they reach that acceptance of this change in their lives. A certain amount of clarity and level-headedness will go a long way toward getting you through to the other side of your divorce.

A lot of factors determine how well you, or your attorney on your behalf, can negotiate for the most satisfactory result in your case. Sometimes there are obstacles to the best possible outcome for you that are things you can affect only a little bit or not at all. Perhaps you cannot make an impact on your spouse's totally unreasonable personality, for example. But some factors that determine how good a result you will get *are* things over which you have at least some control. Paying special attention to factors you *can* have impact on will almost certainly make a difference in whether you come out of your separation sorely wounded, or relatively less injured, emotionally and financially.

Several things that greatly influence the outcome in every divorce case are also things that most people can influence but many people nevertheless overlook, namely: (1) how much each side understands about the substance of the law of property distribution, custody and support; (2) how much information each side has access to; (3) the extent to which each side can treat separation and divorce as a business transaction, as opposed to a continuation of the personality conflicts that resulted in the separation in the first place; and (4) how skillful each side is in negotiations.

If you and your spouse both understand what would probably happen if your case were to be decided by a judge, you will both more likely be able to agree about property distribution, custody and support. The standards used by a judge for deciding custody, support and property issues is the legislative, public definition of what is fair and equitable. To an extent, these detailed, highly evolved and often complicated legal standards allow lawyers to make generally accurate predictions about possible trial outcomes. This is why it matters that each side understands the substance of the law. Each side will measure its own position on custody, support and property according to a prediction of what a judge would most likely do. Only a fool will hold out for a position that is absolutely unobtainable in the courtroom setting.

Similarly, your negotiations will go far more smoothly (and inexpensively, if a lawyer is assisting you) if you can negotiate matter-of-factly, without letting personal issues intrude and sidetrack or distract you. This is why it matters that you resist the temptation to replay your personal animosities with your spouse over every point that comes up as you try to settle the issues arising from your separation.

Although it is unlikely that you will end up in court in a contested divorce, the shadow of a court proceeding looms over almost all divorce negotiations. It is therefore important to have some insight into what will happen if your case actually goes to trial. Bear in mind that you and your spouse can choose to settle at any point in this process; we have had many cases settle at the eleventh hour, sometimes even a mere hour or two before the trial was due to begin.

In most of our cases, it is difficult to define exactly where the early information-gathering process merges with the negotiation process, and where both of those processes turn into trial preparation. There's a great deal of overlap. But in general, there are a number of steps involved in preparing for a trial.

First of all, you and your attorney will go through discovery, as will your spouse and his or her attorney. Discovery is the information-exchanging process of a legal proceeding. In other words, it's the stage at which your attorney is finding out every relevant detail about you, your spouse, and your situation. Some of this will be in the form of documents that you will gather, some will be affidavits submitted by you or your spouse, and some will come in a more structured format, including interrogatories and depositions.

Interrogatories are the written questions served by the opposing party that must be answered in writing as part of the discovery process. You will both be expected to fill out a set of interrogatories, answering the questions completely and truthfully. These can be considered evidence by the judge, so take them seriously. Depositions are the verbal, face-to-face part of discovery—the opposing party counsel asks you questions with your attorney present. Like interrogatories, depositions are considered legal evidence, so you will have to swear not to perjure yourself, just as you would in court. Depositions can also be pretty grueling; both attorneys are trying to get as much information (potentially damning information) as they can, so consider the deposition to be a small taste of what the trial itself will be like.

During the trial, your attorney will have the opportunity to present the testimony of expert witnesses, where applicable. For instance, if you are claiming that your spouse is mentally unstable and therefore shouldn't have custody of your children, your attorney will arrange for one or more mental health experts to testify regarding their examinations of your spouse. Similarly, the housing or business appraisers that we discussed in earlier chapters may be called upon to offer evidence in an equitable distribution trial.

Remember, also, that non-expert witnesses are also likely to be called, and consider the toll this may take on the people in your life, and your relationships with them. In particular, if you are fighting over custody arrangements, will your children themselves be called upon to testify? Attorneys and judges usually try pretty hard not to involve children in legal proceedings, assuming that the experience of being questioned in a courtroom would be too traumatic for most kids, but it can happen. Other people who have a regular role in your life are also fair game: teachers, pastors, neighbors, business associates, and relatives can all be *required* to appear in court. Bear this in mind as you are debating whether or not to settle before you reach the litigation stage.

The trial itself will take place, obviously, in a courtroom, with a judge presiding. The judge's role is particularly significant in a divorce proceeding, because if they go to court, divorce cases are decided by judges, not juries. It is therefore useful, at this point, to briefly consider the judge's role in your case.

You generally will not have any say in which judge hears your case. This creates uncertainty, which should give you and your spouse further incentive to settle without going to court. Furthermore, judges in different parts of a state may interpret the laws differently. You can't be quite sure how any given judge will perceive the evidence presented.

Part of what you pay a lawyer for is his or her knowledge of what judges will do. Be careful, though, about relying too heavily on the opinion of one expert. Judges are often not as predictable as lawyer would like. A judge's decision in a divorce case is usually final; appeals are possible but they are limited and costly.

Judges generally seem to prefer to reach their decisions in private; most will take major issues *under advisement*, meaning that they'll think about it and let your attorney know when they've made a decision. Most rulings are verbal; you'll either return to court to hear what the judge has to say, or, more likely, the judge will call your attorney to give his or her pronouncement. The two attorneys (yours and your spouse's) will then draft the appropriate paperwork, based on the judge's decree, and the two of you, as well as the judge, will sign off on it. The resulting document is a court order, and remains in effect until a judge decides otherwise. Any changes you want to make down the road will have to be effected in court, with the approval of a judge.

In our experience, the adversarial process works very well for people who no longer have to have a relationship when their case is done. Going to court can be very effective for those people, but takes a long time. By the same token, the litigation process hurts people who need to have an intimate relationship over the long haul. Remember: *taking your spouse to court will never resolve your conflicts.* In most divorces, the real conflict is about communication of values or emotions or different parenting styles. All a judge can do is decide on a schedule or a payment amount. The real problems—the fundamental disagreements—can't be resolved in a courtroom. If you have children with this person, you are forever linked by your love for your children. If, for instance, years down the road, you want your children to attend an important event with you (a wedding, perhaps, or a family reunion), your ex isn't necessarily going to just happily switch weekends with you after living through a protracted court battle over that visitation schedule. You are always going to need something from that other parent; what is the best way to get through your divorce, to a place where you can co-parent amicably?

# Finalizing the Divorce

The final, and sometimes incidental, piece of the process is the divorce itself. The ultimate goal of all of this legal wrangling is to get a legal change made to your marital status—this legal change must be documented in a divorce decree, signed by a judge, and filed with the court system. Just like a marriage license or birth certificate, this is recorded with the state, thus making you an officially divorced person.

States differ pretty widely in terms of how the actual divorce (as opposed to issues like alimony, property distribution, custody, etc.) is handled. In many states, the divorce is rolled into the package of attendant issues, and you will automatically receive a divorce decree when your other agreements or orders are finalized. In other states, the divorce decree is a distinct legal proceeding, and must be handled separately from the other issues. In some parts of the country there are even laws that regulate the timing of when issues can be considered relative to the issuance of the divorce decree. Ultimately, while the moment when you receive your copy of the document declaring you to be divorced may be anticlimactic, it's a necessary step along the path to a new life.

# Part Four:
# After the Divorce

# Life after Divorce

## When the Fight Continues

For many of our clients, receipt of the divorce decree closes the door on an unpleasant chapter in their lives. But for many others, the disputes and disagreements continue for years to come. If there are children involved, particularly, you need to recognize that you will, of necessity, be involved in some sort of relationship with your ex for the foreseeable future. With that involvement can come the potential for prolonged conflict, or the potential for substantive personal growth and improved relationship skills. It is often said that the opposite of love is not hatred, but indifference. For many recently divorced people, the hurt and anger are so close to the surface that any interaction with their former spouse can break open old wounds. We urge all of our clients to move into this new phase in their lives ready to improve their relationship skills and learn new methods of conflict resolution.

In the immediate post-divorce period, there may be a number of business details that need to be taken care of in order to fully dissolve the financial aspects of your marriage. You may need to transfer property from one to the other, or remove one person's name from deeds or titles. Wills and estate plans may need to be reconfigured. One or both of you may need to make insurance changes. A dependent spouse has the option, under COBRA, of paying for coverage under the supporting spouse's health insurance plan for up to eighteen months after the marriage ends, but he or she will need to spend those eighteen months finding an alternative that will be in place and activated when the COBRA policy ends. At the same time, auto insurance, homeowners' or renters' policies, disability, or life insurance policies will need to be changed or rewritten to reflect the new, unmarried status of both parties.

If, as part of your divorce, you received a portion of a retirement plan that required a QDRO, make sure to stay on top of the plan administrator to ensure the division is done in a timely manner. Then, do not forget to transfer the assets to an appropriate account for your benefit. If you were not the record keeper in your marriage, you will need to (quickly) establish a system for keeping track of your financial transactions and status; this can be a huge undertaking for some people. At the same time, you may need to learn how to live on a budget, and establish your own credit history. Some of these tasks are merely daunting, but some of them are going to require interaction with your ex-spouse, and for some people, this interaction can be incredibly difficult.

There are generally three areas of potential conflict that can continue to be volatile long after the divorce is final: support (both alimony and child support), custody, and parenting. The first two are clearly issues that, for most people, have been resolved once already, in the form of a settlement agreement or a court-ordered arrangement. It is really best, for everyone involved (including your kids and yourself), that you abide by whatever guidelines were established at the time of your divorce. Failure to comply with the agreement that you signed can only cause you more problems down the road.

When it comes to child support, for instance, many noncustodial parents fail to consistently pay what it costs to provide for the well-being of their children, without really considering the impact on the kids themselves. You've heard of "deadbeat dads"—that's because, as we pointed out earlier, even though most people agree to provide support for their children, many fail to follow through over the long term. This is often due to dissatisfaction with other aspects of the agreement, most frequently the visitation schedule. Nonpayment is a bad idea that could create immediate problems and affect any efforts to modify support in the future. This is the point in your adult life when you have to step back and look at the long-term impact of your actions. If you were ordered or have agreed to pay $500 per month in child support, do the right thing by your children—pay it. Be a grown-up, put aside whatever grudge you have against your ex, and meet your obligation.

There are occasions when the amount indicated by the child support agreement can be changed, and we have found that people are sometimes shocked when they suddenly start receiving a smaller amount each month. They think of the money as something that will continue forever unchanged. However, if the payer loses his or her job, becomes disabled, or dies, the child support will likely be reduced or stopped. In some states (North Carolina is one) the child support agreement can be a contract between the spouses rather than a court order. If the contract does not allow for modification without the agreement of both parties, a payer whose income drops could have assets seized.

If, however, you find yourself on the other side of a child support problem, you need to think carefully about how to address the situation without further escalating tensions. While it might be tempting to withhold visitation until the child support is paid up, you need to remember that the one is not dependent on the other—just as our relationships with our kids are not dependent on our financial circumstances. Try to set the mature example, and remember that your ex is still your child's parent, and your child still needs him or her. If you have a real problem getting the support payments, go through the legal system. If your state's child support enforcement agency seems too backed up or bureaucratic, hire an attorney (either the one who helped you initially, or someone new, if you prefer). In some states you may even be able to find a private child support enforcement firm that specializes in tracking down deadbeat parents and taking legal steps to enforce payment (taking out liens, garnishing wages, etc.). Whatever route you choose to follow, try to distinguish between your need for payment and your anger over the divorce—that anger is not productive, and can really damage your children.

Alimony is a slightly different issue, in that the clear ethical obligation to support is not the same when you're talking about an adult (as opposed to a child). As a result, the legal system is not as deeply committed to enforcing payment of alimony—there are no agencies devoted exclusively to pursuing people who fail to meet their spousal support obligations. Nonetheless, it is in your best interests to treat the issue of alimony as a *financial* matter, not an opportunity for retribution or a way to prolong contact. You wouldn't try to manipulate the phone company as a way to get your emotional needs met—don't try to manipulate your alimony agreement, either. If you need to change the amount, hire an attorney. If the payments aren't being made, again, hire an attorney. That is the best way we know of to keep the interactions civilized—get a neutral third party involved, and get your emotional baggage out of the way.

Child custody—the second post-divorce conflict area—can be an issue fraught with *semantic* conflict that we talked about earlier, even when the reality is ticking along quite smoothly. People often get caught up in labels like "joint custody" and "sole custody," when what they really need to pay attention to is the calendar and the well-being of the children. What matters is the quality time you spend with your children, and the cooperative parenting you do even when you're not with them. As children get older, particularly, they need two parents to be involved in decisions, rules, consequences, and just generally teaching them how to grow up. If your children are small when you get divorced, you'll want to lay the groundwork early on for regular, consistent involvement in their lives. Don't worry about what that involvement is called—just do it.

There is one issue, in particular, that sometimes threatens the stability of a custody arrangement that was agreed upon during separation: when one (or both) parents start dating again. Your spouse's discovery of your interest in another woman or man (as the case may be) could unravel a precarious custody arrangement. The sudden or unexpected appearance of another "parent" figure in your child's life is often experienced as a threatening disruption by the child's other biological parent (or even your ex-spouse's parents), and many people react to such a threat by insisting that the child be totally insulated from a new girl- or boyfriend. While this insistence may be highly unrealistic, its frequent result is to upset a couple's custody plans. Whether your custody plans were once agreed on and are now coming apart because of a new dating partner, or whether there never were any formalized plans, your spouse could try to use the presence of a new person in your life as a "weapon" against your gaining custody of your child or against your continuing to have custody. Appellate cases in some states have rejected this sort of attack, based on the particular facts of those cases. But if your spouse could show that your dating—even unaccompanied by sexual intercourse—had led to distraction or a great preoccupation with your love life, and consequent neglect or inattention to your child, your position in a custody dispute could be greatly weakened.

Dating can present some other "sticky" issues, as well, even if your custody situation is rock-solid. You will eventually have to think through what you are going to tell your children regarding your new romantic relationship(s). As parents, we tend to want to shield our children from too much exposure to sex on television and in movies, but it can be really difficult to clarify our values when the sex/romance in question is our own. Obviously, the age of the child is going to impact how you handle this situation, but this is another area of potential disagreement with your ex that can get really ugly. It is crucial that you approach this particular conversation with your child *as a parent*, rather than as a wounded ex-spouse.

By the same token (the best interests of the children), it is crucial—perhaps even more so than when you were married—that you and your ex learn to function together as a parenting team. Children of divorce quickly learn how to divide and conquer their parents; when those parents don't communicate, or communicate only by shouting at each other, the children figure out how to use the gaps to their advantage. Many kids also realize that their parents feel guilty about the disruption to their lives, and they learn to press those guilt buttons to get their own way or circumvent rules. Remember that even though you and your former spouse no longer live together, you are still co-parents, and you need to work *together* to ensure that your children are growing up in a safe, stable, and healthy environment.

Parenting is hard work, no matter what your marital status; for the sake of your children, try to support each other to fill in the gaps. You will have to interact with each other via the children for many years to come (visualize college graduations, weddings, grandchildren), so for everyone's sake, you should do whatever work you need to now (therapy, behavior modification, medication, etc.) to enable yourself to have a civilized long-term relationship with your ex.

Beyond questions of parenting, there will be other sticky moments when you have no choice but to adjust your relationship with your former spouse. One or both of you will start dating again, or even remarry. No matter how much you believe you are over your marriage, the knowledge that your ex is involved with someone else is going to bring up some emotions. For many people, this is the moment when it becomes clear that they need to get professional help to move beyond this relationship.

For others, that realization doesn't come until they have started dating again themselves. Dating after a long time in a monogamous relationship can be a grand adventure, a chance to learn from past mistakes, or just another series of failed relationships. Whether or not you take this opportunity to learn and grow and become a healthier person is up to you— *you have a choice.* Research shows that second marriages are far more likely to fail than first marriages. We, as a firm, strongly advise our clients to work on the issues that brought them to our office in the first place before becoming a second-marriage statistic. And yes, there have been clients that we've represented in more than one divorce. Serial marriage is neither a healthy nor happy way to go through life. Learn the lessons of your first divorce.

Divorce is never easy and it's rarely pleasant. It does, however, present endless opportunities for personal growth. Some perceive the challenges of divorce as entirely negative. They see each upset, each issue, as something that wears them down. Others view every challenge as an opportunity for growth. They know that overcoming the latest obstacle will make them stronger and more capable. Divorce is difficult. Understanding the opportunity for growth is the key to a smart divorce..

# About the Authors

## Who is Lee Rosen?

Lee Rosen has worked as a divorce lawyer for nearly thirty years. He has mediated, collaborated, negotiated, and litigated thousands of family law matters to successful conclusion. He has consistently been at the leading edge of bringing advanced technological and management approaches to the practice of family law. His work has been recognized by the American Bar Association. Lee has served in a variety of capacities in many organizations, including the National Council of Juvenile and Family Court Judges, the North Carolina Bar Association, and the International Academy of Collaborative Professionals.

## Who is Lisa Angel?

Lisa Angel is a board certified family law specialist and has practiced as a divorce attorney for over twenty years. She has served in leadership capacities for the North Carolina Bar Association and served as chair of the Domestic Violence Commission of North Carolina. She has served as a guest lecturer on family law issues at Duke Law School and University of North Carolina School of Law.

Made in the USA
Charleston, SC
03 February 2015